HUMANIST READINGS IN JEWISH FOLKLORE

HUMANIST READINGS IN JEWISH FOLKLORE

BENNETT MURASKIN

IISHJ & MILAN PRESS

Humanist Readings in Jewish Folklore
©2001
International Institute for Secular Humanistic Judaism
and
Milan Press

Farmington Hills, Michigan

ISBN: 0-9673259-5-1

Cover design by Tracey Rowens
Cover photo: Ketubbah, Padua, Italy 1732
© the Israel Museum, Jerusalem,
used with the permission of the Israel Museum

Table of Contents

Foreword ix

Introduction 1

Chapter I. Talking Back to God 9

Rachel Teaches God a Lesson in Compassion 9

Moses Reasons with God in Defense of the Jewish People 11

... and Demands His Due 14

Questioning God's Justice 15

Resisting God's Will 17

The Angels Resist God, Too 19

Questioning God's Handiwork 20

The Rabbis Overrule God 20

The Light Side: Suing God 22

Chapter II. Confronting Injustice 25

Non-Cooperation 25

Outwitting the Oppressor 27

The Courage to Criticize 35

Korah: Demagogue or Dissident? 36

Defying Illegitimate Authority 39

How to Administer Justice 44

Is There a Right Choice? 46

The Story of the Golem: the Defender of the Jews 48

Chapter III. Mentshlekhkayt (Human Decency) 53

The Primacy of Ethical Behavior 55

Gaining Entrance to Heaven 55

The Difference Between Heaven and Hell 67

In this world too, it's ethical behavior, not piety, that makes a
mentsh: 68

Standing Up for Your Rights 75

A Hasidic Folktale 78

Respecting Other Opinions 82
Patience 83
Rabbi Meir Learns from a Heretic, a.k.a., an Apikoros 85

Chapter IV. The Rich and the Poor 87

Why Sodom Was Destroyed 87
What Causes Plagues to Strike 88
Homeless in Imperial Rome 89
Justice for the Worker and the Poor 89
Respect for the Dignity of the Worker and the Poor 94
Maimonides' Eight Degrees of Charity 97
Helping Those in Need 99
What's Worse than Not Helping 103
How to Deal with Skinflints 104
... and with a "Welfare Cheat" 105
The Light Side: The Miracle of the Broken Leg 106

Chapter V. The Dangers of Fanaticism 107

The Destruction of the Second Temple 107
Life Must Go On 111
Wrong Priorities 114

Chapter VI. Jewish Humor 115

Poking Fun at the Pious 116
The Witty vs. the Wealthy 121
The Disputation 127
Dying to Get In 130
Gratitude for Small Favors (or He Got Off Easy) 131
A Lesson in Hospitality 132
Chutzpa 132

Chapter VII. Women 137

Lilith, the First Feminist 137
Leah Turns the Tables on Jacob 139

A Rabbinical Sage Learns the Law from His Wife 140
Take Your Choice: Wealth, Learning,
    or a Virtuous Woman 140
Heroism and Sacrifice 143
The Story of Susanna 145
Wisdom Before Beauty 149
You've Come a Long Way, Skotsl 150
The Light Side: The Rabbi and the Rebbitzen 152

Chapter VIII. Jewish-Gentile Relations 153

Abraham and the Heathen 153
Ishmael, the Disfavored Son, Is Judged to Be Righteous 155
A Midrash on Racism 156
A Jew Comes to the Aid of a Roman 158
A Roman Comes to the Aid of a Jew 161
The Rabbi and the Emperor 163
A Pagan Fulfills the Fifth Commandment ... and More 165
Dealing Honestly with All People 166
Good Neighbors 167
The Gentiles Were Angels 169

Chapter IX. The Value of Education 171

Respect for Learning 171
... and Teachers 172
Scholarship Is the Most Valuable Merchandise 173
But There Are Alternatives to Bible and Talmud Study 174
How to Teach an Unwilling Student 174

Chapter X. Parents & Children 179

Honor Thy Father and Thy Mother 179
A Parents' Responsibility 182
Respect for the Elderly (or Teach Your Children Well) 183

Chapter XI. Friendship 187

Chapter XII. The Sanctity of Human Life 191

Chapter XIII. The Evil of Slander 195
... and a Humane Cure 196

Chapter XIV. Some Humanistic Principles to Live By
from Pirke Avot 197
And Finally 198

Chapter XV. Why Remain Jewish? 199

Acknowledgments 201

Bibliography 207

Author's Note on Sources 211

Afterword 217

Foreword

The culture of ordinary people can be extraordinary.

Living at this moment in history, we enjoy the openness of our intellectual culture—no longer limited exclusively to elite sources, we now draw inspiration and historical continuity from the creativity of ordinary people to a degree not supported by previous generations. While the Romantic movement in the 18th and 19th centuries tied folklore to political nationalism and the essence of the *volk* (people), secular Jews who recorded East European Jewish folklore at the turn of the 20th century were often mining for something else: a well-spring for a modern cultural Jewish identity. To base one's Jewishness on a broader understanding of Jewish culture, and not just on the elite sources of Talmudic law and rabbinic discourse, was a first step towards a Jewish identity based on the diversity of the Jewish experience.

What was an act of preservation in Eastern Europe 100 years ago and in Israel over the last 60 years can now be a source of inspiration for Secular Humanistic Judaism. This work by Bennett Muraskin, a well-respected public intellectual in the secular Jewish movement for many years, has taken some of the best Jewish folklore preserved by previous generations and made it available, accessible and meaningful. One of the missions of the International Institute for Secular Humanistic Judaism is to publish materials of interest and inspiration to secular, cultural and Humanistic Jews, and this work meets that mission admirably.

There are two particular nuggets of wisdom underlying this publication. First, Muraskin realizes that we need more roots than only

the past few centuries since the Enlightenment, but also that our
more ancient roots in the Bible and most of rabbinic literature are
complicated for Secular Humanistic Jews to use. When we cite
these latter sources, we have to explain their context, take them
out of context, or otherwise mediate the fact that, even when the
ethical values expressed agree with ours, they were written by
individuals whose lifestyle and beliefs differed vastly from our own.
In Jewish folklore, on the other hand, we have both literature
whose origins lie centuries before our own and whose relevance
to our way of life is very clear. Indeed, it is satisfying to find many
examples of this folklore—this "underground tradition"—in the central documents of rabbinic Judaism such as Talmud and Midrash.

Even more important, Muraskin is wise enough to avoid the "god-
allergy" that all too often afflicts framers of secular Judaism. Some
who have left or react against a religious tradition become so allergic to the word "god" that they seemingly cannot bear to hear or
read the word in any other than a negative setting. So they rewrite
Biblical stories to eliminate Yahveh, the God of the Hebrews, having Moses part the Red Sea by magic rather than Yahveh's miracle. And they reject any folk tales where characters genuinely talk
and pray to God, and sometimes where God answers back.

Muraskin, in both his Introduction and his astute choice of readings, clearly understands the difference between a philosophical or
liturgical affirmation of theological belief, which Secular and
Humanistic Jewish communities avoid, and the use of "God" as a
character in myth and folklore. No one is allergic to reading about
Zeus; they do not feel their secularism threatened.

Why not treat Yahveh, the God of Jewish tradition, as we do
Zeus? Why not treat Jewish folklore, which began before
Enlightenment was a twinkle in Spinoza's eye, as the continued
myths of the Jewish people? Most important, we today can find
inspiration from historic themes in Jewish folklore like talking back
to God, confronting injustice, *mentshlekhkayt* (human decency),
the dangers of fanaticism, and every other chapter in this collec-

tion; they are not identical to our approach, but they are clearly evolutionary forebears just the same.

There is a Jewish tradition of another writer providing a *hakdama*, an introduction to and endorsement of the volume at hand. What today are blurbs on book jackets were for our ancestors invitations to begin reading. Having learned from, studied with and taught next to Bennett Muraskin, I am very proud to carry on that tradition. Now, come and study!

Rabbi Adam Chalom
Dean, North America
International Institute for
Secular Humanistic Judaism

Introduction

Secular Humanistic Jews often have difficulty finding Jewish literature written before the *Haskala* (Jewish Enlightenment) that reflects their beliefs. This is understandable because Jewish secularism did not exist as an alternative to rabbinic Judaism until two hundred years ago.

Some Secular Humanistic Jews have attempted to extract humanistic messages from the Bible using the art of selective quotation. This is a risky business because the Bible's central message is profoundly authoritarian and ethnocentric. Even the Prophets express many ideas that we would find intolerable if we ever took the trouble to read more than a few excerpts about peace and justice. For instance, since they all claim to have a direct line to God, they categorically reject any dissenting opinions. There are exceptional books in the Bible that have powerful humanist messages, specifically Jonah, Ruth, Ecclesiastes, the Song of Songs and Job, but they are rarely given the attention they deserve in either Jewish religious or secular circles.

On the other hand, if we limit ourselves to those Jewish thinkers who rejected theistic Judaism completely, there would be almost no one to cite until Spinoza in the seventeenth century. There *were* isolated freethinkers (*apikorsim*) such as Elisha ben Abuyah, a Talmudic sage from the second century C.E., and Hiwi Al-Balkhi, a Persian philosopher from the tenth century, but none of their heretical writings have survived. More importantly, they left no disciples.

Sherwin Wine, an outstanding Secular Humanistic Jewish thinker, observes that Jews derived their humanistic values not from religious texts, but from their experience as an urbanized world people who chafed under rabbinic authority. This experience, he comments, was

reflected in the "underground folk tradition: Its heroes are the angry mockers of authority who conform reluctantly because they
have to — and who are more comfortable when laughing than
praying." They express anger at the world's injustice, skepticism
toward religious dogma and an ironic sense of humor.

Where can we find this tradition? Although Wine sees Jewish
humor as its repository, his overall conclusion is that Jewish humanists do *not* have their own literature prior to the Haskala because the rabbis suppressed it.

In my view, there *is* a place where the underground folk tradition
comes to the surface — in Jewish folklore. Some of it comes from
the Talmud — not from the legalistic portion, called *Halakha*, but
from the non-legalistic portion, called *Aggada*, which constitutes
an alternative to Talmudic law. It consists of parables, legends
and imaginative reinterpretations of Bible stories. It also includes
Pirke Avot (Sayings of the Fathers), which is widely recognized
as the Talmud's most accessible exposition of ethical values.
Beyond *Aggada*, there is *Midrash*, another excellent rabbinic
source of parables, legends and folktales created over many centuries throughout the early Middle Ages. There is also an abundance of folklore from Yiddish (especially Hasidic), Hebrew and
other Jewish sources reflecting both the Ashkenazic and Sephardic
traditions.

Within this vast body of literature, there are many stories that
clearly express essential humanistic values. They teach us to
question authority, resist injustice and respect human dignity within
a Jewish cultural/religious context.

In Jewish folklore, one can find Mother Rachel teaching God compassion, rabbis challenging God's injustice, freethinkers questioning conventional pieties and ordinary Jews defying unjust laws.
Exploiters of the poor are castigated, religious fanaticism is de-
nounced and the virtues of *mentshlekhkayt* are elevated over ritual

observances. There is plenty of humor too. This is a rich source of Jewish humanism that we ought to tap.

Secular Jews have always been drawn to Jewish folklore. Chaim Zhitlovsky (1865-1943), one of our seminal thinkers, praised it in these terms: "The God of Jewish legend ... the God of the *Aggada* is a humanized God," he wrote. "All the narratives, from the *Aggada* to the last Hasidic fantastic story, contain so much pure human beauty ... that even the soul of an atheist can be inspired by them. ..."

S. Ansky (1863-1920), the great Yiddish short story writer and dramatist, who collected Jewish folklore from the Ukraine, described it as a new Torah for the Jewish masses. Two of the people chiefly responsible for collecting Jewish folklore for the modern reader, Chaim Nachman Bialik (1873-1934), the great Hebrew poet, and his collaborator, Yehoshua Ravnitsky (1859-1944), were attracted by its ethical content. The Hebrew writer Micha Joseph Berdichevsky (1865-1921), also known as Micha Joseph bin Gurion, was a secularist influenced by romanticism. He collected Jewish folklore because he saw it as the ultimate expression of Jewish dissent and diversity.

Other luminaries have been drawn to Jewish folklore as well. Martin Buber (1878-1965), the great humanistic religious philosopher, was inspired by the egalitarian message of early Hasidism to publish two volumes of Hasidic tales. The person most responsible for making Jewish folklore available to the American Jewish public — Nathan Ausubel (1899-1986), author of *A Treasury of Jewish Folklore* — consistently displayed strong humanistic tendencies in his work. Another great folklorist, American Jewish scholar Louis Ginzberg (1873-1953), was deeply religious In the traditional sense. Yet he recognized in Jewish folklore the authentic voices of the Jewish common people.

On the other hand, Raphael Patai (1910-1996) an outstanding contemporary Jewish scholar and folklorist, asserts that Jewish folklore is basically reverential. He argues that "... almost all the biblical heroes and later Jewish heroes conform to this single pattern: They are heroes of piety, giants of belief, masters of obedience. Their one and only heroic act is to perceive and obey God's command."

I do not share this view. Although much Jewish folklore falls within this framework, there is another tradition struggling to be heard. It is the one that stresses the role of human volition. Impiety, disbelief and defiance also have their place and are especially worth preserving, when wedded to a commitment to social justice, respect for women and Gentiles and high ethical standards. In Yiddish, we call this the quest for a *besere un shenere velt* (a better and more beautiful world); in Hebrew, *tikkun olam* (repair of the world).

Should it concern us that many of these stories appear in a religious garb? Being a Secular Humanistic Jew does not mean discarding everything that is expressed in religious language. It would be impossible to read a page of the classic Yiddish writers I.L. Peretz (1852-1915) and Sholem Aleichem (1859-1916) or Hebrew literary pathfinders Ahad Ha'am (1856-1927) and Chaim Bialik without appreciating how religious themes profoundly contributed to secular Yiddish and Hebrew culture. As Lucy Dawidowicz (1917-1992), a prominent Jewish historian, commented, "Jewish folklore, steeped in ancient Jewish religious traditions in which rabbinic, hasidic and secular motifs were intermingled, helped enrich secular Yiddish and Hebrew literature and culture."

By embracing Jewish folklore, the movement for Secular Humanistic Judaism and Secular Jewishness can link itself to the *goldene kayt* (golden chain) of Jewish tradition that Jewish humanism, both secular and religious, played an indispensable role in creating.

The author wishes to thank the following people for their assistance in the preparation of this book: my wife, Ellen Muraskin, Eli

Rubenstein, Karen Levy, Jeff Zolitor, Barry Dancis and Wallace Green. I want to thank my editor Bonnie Cousens. Special thanks go to Marilyn Rowens, who saw this project through to completion, and Ron Milan, who provided the indispensable financial support. Finally, I wish to recognize the late Max Rosenfeld, who introduced me to the world of Jewish folklore.

— B.M.

Rabban Simeon Gamaliel said: The world rests on three foundations: truth, justice and peace.
> *— Pirke Avot (Sayings of the Fathers)*

When we seek in our past the sources that should and do water our life and creativity...we should consider their intrinsic worth — whether they have dried up and are empty or whether they are still full and ebullient. From each epoch, each stream, each current in our historic life, we should select those religious and ethical values or those intellectual and artistic achievements that can help bind us to our historical tradition without being bound by it.
> *— Shmuel Niger, literary and social critic (1883-1955)*

Historic Judaism is not only a religion...It is a broad expanse of culture...Judaism is comprised of religious, moral, social, messianic, philosophical and political ideas...so broad and multifaceted that each Jew can choose whatever is in keeping with his convictions.
> *— Simon Dubnow, Russian Jewish historian (1860-1941)*

Chapter I.
Talking Back to God

Throughout our history, Jews have been acutely conscious of the contradiction between their exalted place in the Bible and their insecure place in the real world. Yet, in pre-modern times, most Jews profoundly believed in the sanctity of scripture. This apparent contradiction was addressed in two ways: interpretation and confrontation. This chapter explores the interplay between them.

Beginning with Abraham's appeal to God not to destroy all human life in Sodom and Job's insistence that God had no right to punish an innocent man, Jews have challenged God's moral authority. As recorded in Exodus 32:9-14 and Numbers 14:11-20, only Moses' decisive intervention prevented God from annihilating the entire people of Israel.

Such incidents occur nowhere else in the Bible, yet they are common to Jewish folklore. As S. Ansky, the great Yiddish writer said, "... Jewish folklore creations are about truth and justice. Truth stands so high that it calls even God to judgment. If the Almighty issues a harsh decree, the righteous man comes to nullify it."

Although framed in a religious perspective, this willingness to argue with God gave later generations of Jews the courage to adopt the secular humanist belief in the power of people to transform the world without divine guidance.

Rachel Teaches God a Lesson in Compassion

When the [First] Temple was being destroyed [by the Babylonian Empire in 586 B.C.E.], Abraham came before

God with his garments rent in mourning and with ashes on his head, crying bitterly, "Why did You allow us to be reduced to such shame and derision?" When the ministering angels saw him they too joined him in mourning the tragic fate of Jerusalem.

God turned to the angels and demanded why they had joined together in their complaints. "Because Abraham Your beloved has come into Your house wailing and weeping. Why did You not take care of him?" they challenged.

Abraham then turned to God and asked "O Lord of the Universe! Why have you exiled my children and delivered them into the hands of the gentiles who kill them with brutality? Why have You destroyed the Sanctuary built on the place where I prepared to offer up my son Isaac to You?"

"Because your children have sinned and transgressed against all the Torah," said God.

Moses went forward and added his pleadings, "Oh Lord of the Universe! Was I not a faithful shepherd of this people for forty years, when I pulled them along in the wilderness like a horse? Then when the time came for them at last to enter the Promised Land, You decreed that my bones should remain in the wilderness. But now that they are exiled into the hands of the enemy You bid me come and mourn for them."

Moses then said to Jeremiah "Show me the way and I will go and see who it is who opposed them." Jeremiah responded that it would be impossible to make a way over the numbers of the slain lying on the roads, but Moses insisted.

Moses then went on the way, preceded by Jeremiah, until he came to the rivers of Babylon. When the people saw him, they said to each other "The son of Amram has risen from his grave to redeem us." Then the heavenly voice was heard, "My decree is final."

On his return, Moses reported to the patriarchs on the dire plight of the Jews, how they had been killed, tortured and humiliated by a savage and barbaric enemy. He continued his plea to God and complained of the tragic fate which had befallen his people.

Suddenly, Mother Rachel came forward and said to God, "Lord of the Universe! You full well know that Jacob loved me passionately and labored for my father for seven years so that he could marry me. Then when the time for my marriage came, my father substituted my sister for me. Yet I was not jealous of my sister and did not shame her. Now if I, who am but flesh and blood, dust and ashes, was not jealous of my adversary, why are You, who are eternal and compassionate, jealous of the idols, which are quite meaningless, and have sent my children into exile?"

Then the compassion of God was awakened and He said "For your sake, Rachel, I will restore Israel to its land."
— *adapted from Hayyim Bialik and Yehoshua Ravnitsky,*
Sefer Ha'Aggadah, The Book of Jewish Folklore and Legend,
selected by Chaim Pearl

From the traditional religious perspective, Jews can only suffer because God wills it. Yet within this tradition, it is recognized that human beings can challenge God's authority. Here, the angels themselves join with some of the greatest heroes of the Bible (Abraham, Moses and Jeremiah) to appeal to God's sense of compassion, but only a woman, Rachel is successful. How? She presents her response to a humiliating experience in her personal life as a model for God to follow in deciding the fate of the Jewish people!

Moses Reasons with God
in Defense of the Jewish People

In the Book of Exodus, the Hebrews built a golden calf while waiting for Moses to come down from Mt. Sinai. God was so furious at them for resorting to idol worship that He threatened to wipe them out completely. However, Moses intervened and convinced God to relent. The rabbis provided a number of explanations of how he did it.

Why does Your anger blaze forth against Your people whom you delivered from the land of Egypt? (Exod. 32:11).

Why did Moses have to mention here the Exodus from Egypt? Merely to remind God "Lord of the Universe! From where did You take them? From Egypt, of course, where everyone worshipped animals!"

Moses said to God, "Lord of the Universe! You ignored the whole world and chose Egypt, the land where the people worship lambs, as the place where Your children would be in servitude. Naturally, they learned from the Egyptians and so came to make the golden calf." That is why Moses stressed the land of Egypt, as if to say, "Consider where You brought them from!"

Our rabbis taught: When Moses went up on high, he saw God sitting and writing the words *slow to anger (Num. 14:18)*. Moses asked God, "Does this mean that You are slow to anger to the good people?" and God replied, "Even to the wicked." Moses was astonished, "Let the wicked perish!" he said. And God answered "The time will come when this special forbearance will be needed."

When Israel sinned with the golden calf, God said to Moses, "Didn't you say to me that forbearance should be extended only towards the righteous?" In reply Moses said, "But didn't You promise that Your patience would be applied also to the wicked?"

— adapted from Bialik and Ravnitzky,
Sefer Ha-Aggadah, The Book of Jewish Folklore and Legend,
selected by Chaim Pearl

Moses uses three tactics to defuse God's anger. First, he takes a sociological approach, contending that the bad behavior of the Hebrews is a result of their environment, *i.e.*, Egypt. Second, he blames God for placing the Hebrews in that environment in the first place and, third, he insists that God live up to his own promises. Not bad for a day's work!

> Why does Your anger blaze forth against Your people? (*Ibid.*).

> When the Hebrews in the desert built a golden calf and began to worship it, Moses spoke to God and said: "Lord of the Universe! Why are You annoyed at Your people? They have provided You with an assistant. Can't You see that this calf will be helpful to you? You will make the sun rise and it will make the moon to rise. While You direct the stars, it will take charge of the constellations. You will make the dew fall and it will make the winds blow. You will be responsible for the rains, while it will cause the plants to grow." The Almighty answered, "Moses, you are even more confused than the people, because you must know that the calf has none of these powers." "If that is so," Moses responded, "why does Your anger blaze forth against Your people?"
> — *adapted from Midrash, Exodus Rabbah 43:6*

As in the previous stories in this chapter, Moses sets an excellent precedent for generations of Jews who needed a great deal of cleverness to outwit their enemies. This is a side of Moses that has a much greater appeal to humanists than his traditional role as giver of the Law.

⌘⌘⌘

In Exodus, God decrees that the sins of the fathers will be inherited by their sons, but in Deuteronomy, He declares that each person is responsible for his own sins. Since these two state-

ments are contradictory, Moses is given credit for convincing God
to adopt the second, more humane approach.

> When the Holy One, blessed be He, said to Moses: "... visit-
> ing the iniquity of the fathers upon the children" (Exod. 20:5),
>
> Moses said: Many are the wicked who have begotten righ-
> teous children; shall they take the consequences of their
> fathers' iniquities?
>
> Terah served images, and Abraham, his son, was righteous;
> the same with Hezekiah who was righteous, and Ahaz his
> father wicked, the same with Josiah who was righteous and
> Amon his father wicked. Is it right then that the righteous be
> struck down for the iniquity of their fathers?
>
> The Holy One, blessed be He, said: By your life, I am voiding
> my words and fulfilling yours.
>
> As it is said: "The fathers shall not be put to death for the children,
> neither shall the children be put to death for the fathers"
> (*Deut. 24:16*).
>
> > — *from Nahum N. Glatzer, Ed.,*
> > *Hammer on the Rock, A Short Midrash Reader*

... and Demands His Due

In the Torah, God decrees that Moses must die without the honor
of setting foot on the Promised Land because of some trivial of-
fense he committed in the desert. Moses is understandably indig-
nant.

> Master of the Universe, You well know how much I have
> endured in attempting to make the people of Israel believe in
> You and obey Your laws. I assumed that because I have
> shared in their misfortunes, You would allow me to share
> their reward. But now that You have decided that the people
> of Israel will finally receive their reward, You say to me,

"You shall not cross over Jordan" (*Deut. 31:2*).

I declare that You violate Your own Torah, because it is
written: "You must pay the worker his wages on the same day
before the sun sets, for he is needy and urgently depends on it;
or else he will cry to the Lord against you and you will incur
guilt" (*Deut. 24:15*). Is this the reward I deserve for my forty
years of labor to make Israel into a holy people?
             — *adapted from Midrash, Deuteronomy Rabbah 11:10*

The answer from God? Yes, it is.

Questioning God's Justice

On the evening of the Day of Atonement, Rabbi Levi
Yitzchok of Berditchev, "the poor man's rabbi," asked an
illiterate tailor, "Since you couldn't read the prayers today,
what did you say to God?"

"I said to God," replied the tailor, "Dear God, You want me to
repent of my sins, but my sins have been so small! I confess: There
have been times when I failed to return to the customers the pieces
of left-over cloth. When I could not help it, I even ate food
that was not kosher. But really, is that so terrible? Now take
Yourself, God! Just examine Your own sins: You have robbed
mothers of their babes, and have left helpless babes orphans.
So You see that Your sins are much more serious than mine.
I'll tell You what, God! Let's make a deal! You forgive me
and I'll forgive You."

"Ah, you foolish man!" cried Rabbi Levi Yitzchok. "You let
God off too easily! Just think! You were in an excellent
position to make Him redeem the whole Jewish people!"
             — *from Nathan Ausubel, A Treasury of Jewish Folklore*

Levi Yitzchok of Berditchev, Poland, a famous Hasidic *rebbe* also
known as the Berditchever Rebbe, lived from 1740 to1809. He
viewed himself as the advocate of the Jewish people in dealing

with a frequently callous, unjust God. Contemporary rabbis take the opposite approach. They assume the role of God's defense attorney, making excuses for all His deficiencies. What place does a non-believer have in this debate? If one views God as the ultimate authority figure, I believe the answer is obvious: Speak truth to power!

⌘⌘⌘

The rabbi was walking along the road when he met a fat rich man who was smoking.

"Why do you smoke? It's an awful vice!" he rebuked him.

"I smoke to help me digest my dinner; I overate," apologized the fat rich man.

Further on the rabbi met a thin poor man who also was smoking.

"Why do you smoke? Don't you know it's a terrible vice?" the rabbi lectured him severely.

"I smoke to drive away the pangs of hunger," murmured the thin poor man apologetically.

"Lord of the World!" cried the rabbi, lifting his eyes to heaven. "Where is Your Justice? If only the fat rich man would give the poor thin man some of his dinner, both of them would be healthier and happier, and neither of them would have to smoke!"
                                        — from Ausubel, A Treasury of Jewish Folklore

It is good to know that anti-smoking activists were depicted in our folklore, but it is even more gratifying to see that Jewish folklore concerns itself with both divine and social injustice.

⌘⌘⌘

Lord of the Universe! I [Rabbi Levi Yitzchok of Berditchev] saw an ordinary Jew pick up his *tefillin* [phylacteries] from the floor and kiss them; and You have left your *tefillin*, the Jewish people, lie on the ground for more than two thousand years, trampled by their enemies. Why do you not pick them up? Why do You not act as a plain Jew acts? Why?
— *from Joseph Telushkin, Jewish Wisdom*

Indeed, it was the more secular-minded Jews who took the future of the Jewish people in their own hands by breaking out of the ghettos and joining democratic, socialist and Zionist movements. Secular Humanistic Jews (along with Reconstructionists), however, do not subscribe to the view that the Jews are the Chosen People.

Resisting God's Will

It chanced once that a great calamity almost befell the Angel of Death. He came pretty near losing the knife with which he severs the life of man. When Rabbi Joshua ben Levi was at the point of death, the Angel of Death came to see him.

"Show me first my place in Paradise," pleaded Rabbi Joshua. "That will make it easier for me to depart from this life."

"Come, I will show you," answered the Angel of Death. And so they ascended to the celestial regions.

On the way, Rabbi Joshua said to the Angel of Death, "Do give me your knife. I am afraid that you will frighten me with it while we are on the way."

The Angel of Death felt pity for him and gave him his knife.

When they at last arrived in Paradise the Angel of Death showed Rabbi Joshua the place reserved for him. A great yearning then seized Rabbi Joshua and he sprang forward within the Gates.

But the Angel of Death seized hold of him by the skirts of his garment and tried to pull him back.

Having the knife in his possession, Rabbi Joshua refused to budge from his place.

"I swear I will not leave Paradise!" he cried.

Thereupon, a great tumult was heard among the angels. It seemed very much as if death was about to be abolished from the world and people would be able to live forever, like the angels.

The Angel of Death stood in a great quandary. "What to do now?" he wondered.

The holy man had solemnly sworn that he would not leave Paradise, and who could violate the oath of such a man? So the Angel of Death went to complain to God Himself. And God said, "I decree that Rabbi Joshua must return to earth. His time has not come yet."

The Angel of Death came again to Rabbi Joshua and demanded in a terrible voice, "Give me back my knife!"

"I will not give it back to you!" cried Rabbi Joshua. "I want to abolish Death forever!"

Suddenly the Voice of God was heard sternly commanding, "Return the knife, Joshua! Man must continue to die!"
                              — *from Ausubel, A Treasury of Jewish Folklore*

Rabbi Joshua ben Levi lived (and died) in Judea in the third century C.E. In this story, he resembles Prometheus, the hero of Greek mythology who stole fire from the heavens. There is also a parallel to the Tower of Babel story. "Storming the heavens" appears to be a powerful human instinct, common to different eras and cultures.

The Angels Resist God, Too

The story is told that the leading men of the community were unsatisfied with the work of the caretaker of Rabbi Yoshe-Ber's rabbinical court in Brisk. They held a meeting and decided to fire the caretaker. Then they gave the task of dismissing him to Rabbi Yoshe-Ber, but he refused.

"Why not, Rabbi?" the community leaders asked. "You're the rabbi and he's your employee."

"I'll tell you," Rabbi Yoshe-Ber replied. "Since you read and know the story of the sacrifice of Isaac, you know that when the Blessed Name commanded Abraham to sacrifice Isaac, we find that it is written that He Himself spoke as follows: 'Take now thy son, thine only son. ...' But when He commanded Abraham to spare Isaac, God sent an angel, as it is written, 'And the angel called unto Abraham. ...'

"This poses a question. Why was it that the Blessed Name did not send an angel at the beginning? The answer is that He knew very well that no angel would have accepted the assignment. Each of them would have said, 'If You want to command death, You had better do it Yourself.'"

— *from Beatrice Silverman Weinreich, Ed., Yiddish Folktales*

This is much more than a story about a rabbi who refused to fire his caretaker at the request of the communal leadership. Abraham's willingness to sacrifice his son, Isaac, known in Hebrew as the *akeda*, is traditionally depicted as a noble act proving Abraham's total devotion of God. Rabbi Yoshe-Ber's response turns that interpretation on its head. The implication is that Abraham should have defied God's order. After all, in Genesis 18:22-32, Abraham mustered the courage to contend with God on behalf of the innocent people of Sodom. Shouldn't he have done at least as much to save the life of his own son?

Questioning God's Handiwork

The rabbi ordered a pair of new pants for the Passover holidays from the village tailor. The tailor, who was very unreliable, took a long time finishing the job. The rabbi was afraid that he would not have the garment ready for the holidays.

On the day before Passover, the tailor came running all out of breath to deliver the pants.

The rabbi examined his new garment with a critical eye.

"Thank you for bringing my pants on time," he said. "But tell me, my friend, if it took God only six days to create our vast and complicated world, why did it have to take you six weeks to make this simple pair of pants?"

"But Rabbi!" murmured the tailor triumphantly, "Just look at the mess God made, and then look at this beautiful pair of pants!"

— from Ausubel, A Treasury of Jewish Folklore

From the perspective of Secular Humanistic Judaism, this story is as Jewish as any passage from the Torah.

The Rabbis Overrule God

The rabbis were discussing the case of "the oven of achnai" — an oven whose sections had been separated and filled with sand between each layer. Rabbi Eliezer said that such an oven is not subject to ritual defilement but all the others disagreed with him. Eliezer gave his colleagues every possible reason why he held his minority view, but his arguments were not accepted.

Finally he said, "If I am right then the carob tree outside will prove it." And they saw that the tree uprooted itself one hundred cubits. Still, the rabbis could not be persuaded.

"Then let the stream of water prove that I am right!" said
Eliezer. And the stream outside the academy changed its
course. But the rabbis refused to accept even that sign.

"In that case," said Eliezer, "let the walls of the school house
vindicate me." And the walls immediately began to fall inwards.
At this Rabbi Joshua rose and rebuked them. "If the scholars
of the academy are debating points of law, what has that got
to do with you?" So the walls did not collapse out of respect
for Rabbi Joshua; neither did they straighten out in deference
to Rabbi Eliezer, but they remained in an inclined position.

Rabbi Eliezer then turned to his colleagues and said, "Then let
the heavens declare that I am right." Whereupon a heavenly
bat kol [voice] was heard to say, "Why do you dispute with
Rabbi Eliezer since the law is rightly in his view?" But Rabbi
Joshua stood firm and proclaimed: "The Torah is not in
heaven (*Deut. 30:12*), so we will not listen even to a *bat kol*.
In any case we have been taught in the Torah itself that we
always follow the majority ruling."

When Rabbi Nathan came across Elijah he asked the prophet,
"Tell me, what was God doing while all that was happening?"
The prophet replied, "God smiled and said, 'My children have
defeated Me.'"
> — *from Bialik and Ravnitsky, Stories of the Sages,*
> *from Sefer Ha'aggadah, selected by Chaim Pearl*

Rabbi Eliezer, whose full name was Eliezer Ben Hyrcanus, was
excommunicated for refusing to accept the majority opinion.

This famous story appears in numerous collections. It relates to a
period in Jewish history when our ancestors created a new way of
being Jewish based on the rule of law.

With the destruction of the Second Temple (70 C.E.) and the defeat of the Bar Kokhba revolt (135 C.E.) that sought to restore it,

the old priestly ruling class was destroyed. Teachers and scholars reconstructed Jewish life on a more egalitarian and tolerant basis.

Even though the matter under debate in this story is quite legalistic, i.e., *pilpul*, the principle that rabbis had the right to democratically overrule "the voice of God" marked a turning point. Talmudic or rabbinic Judaism became the next stage in Jewish life.

Eighteen hundred years after the rabbis overruled God, we believe Judaism has evolved to the point were it can encompass a Judaism without God, rooted in both modern secular ideas and Jewish sources, such as the humanist stories that appear in this collection.

The Light Side: Suing God

A villager once came to see the rabbi in a big town and said to him, Rabbi, I come from a nearby village. I want to bring a lawsuit against God. My reason for it is this. I had a wife and, in addition, ten thousand rubles. What did God do? First he took away the ten thousand rubles and, afterwards, my wife too. I ask you: What would it have mattered to God if He had done the reverse? Had he taken away my wife first I would have remained a widower with ten thousand rubles. In that case it would have been easy for me to have married a woman with a ten-thousand ruble dowry. After that, had God wanted to take from me the ten thousand rubles, I still would have had left a wife and ten thousand rubles."

"Tell me, my friend," asked the rabbi a bit puzzled at all this, "why did you come to me with your suit and not to the rabbi in your village?"

"I'll be perfectly frank with you," replied the villager. "I couldn't trust such a matter to our rabbi because I know what a God-fearing man he is and he would give Him the decision.

On the other hand, I know you have no fear of God and so, at least, I'll have half a chance with you."
— *from Ausubel, A Treasury of Jewish Folklore*

Notice that the rabbi approached to decide a lawsuit against God is the one that lives in a "big town" rather than one from the petitioner's village. Urban culture tends to promote free thought, and the concentration of Jews in cities and large towns helps explain their embrace of modern secular ideas.

Chapter II.
Confronting Injustice

Be cautious in dealing with government officials. ... They pretend to be on your side when it is to their advantage, but you cannot depend on them when you are in trouble.
            — *Rabban Gamaliel from Pirke Avot*

... justice delayed [is] justice perverted.
                                   — *Pirke Avot*

Non-Cooperation

Eleazar once came across a government detective whose job it was to apprehend thieves. "How do you manage to discover the culprits?" Eleazar asked.

"It's not too difficult," said the man. "They live like animals who hide by day and come out at night."

"But perhaps you are arresting the wrong man," said Eleazar. "In fact, you could easily be letting the guilty people go free."

"Well, there is nothing much that I can do about that. I have to do my job as best as I can, and if there are mistakes it just can't be helped."

Rabbi Eleazar said, "Then allow me to suggest to you how you might successfully discover those who are really guilty. You go to a cafe in the middle of the morning and if you see someone there who is dozing over his cup, then make some inquiries about him. If the man is a student, then you may surmise that he rose early to study. If he is a workman then again you can infer that he got up early in order to get to work. But if he is neither then you should arrest him because the chances are that he has been up all night in his thieving pursuits."

The conversation came to the ears of the Roman governor, who said, "Let this man who gave such excellent advice be appointed chief detective."

When Rabbi Joshua ben Korha heard about Eleazar's new job, he protested to him very strongly, "You vinegar, product of wine! How can you send fellow Jews to be punished by the Romans!" Eleazar defended himself and said, "I am only cutting out the thorns from the vineyard." But Joshua rebutted, "Let the owner of the vineyard do his own dirty work; he doesn't need you."

> *— from Bialik and Ravnitsky, Stories of the Sages,*
> *from Sefer Ha'aggadah, selected by Chaim Pearl*

The Eleazar of this story refers to Eleazar ben Simeon, a second century C.E. scholar who turned "informer." Joshua ben Korha, his contemporary, was a Jewish militant.

This story raises a troubling question. To what extent should subject people collaborate with a hostile authority? Joshua ben Korha clearly has the last word when he reprimands Eleazar for joining the Roman police in order to catch thieves. But how can any society function if its members do not actively oppose criminal behavior? Joshua ben Korha's answer appears to be that there should be no collaboration because the Roman authorities were the real criminals. Since Joshua ben Korha lived in the aftermath of the Bar Kokhba revolt (132-135 C.E.), brutally crushed by the Romans, his attitude is understandable. However, in the long term, Jews learned to accommodate themselves to Roman rule and regained a significant degree of autonomy.

⌘ ⌘ ⌘

A man came to Raba and said: "The prefect of my town has
ordered me to kill so and so, or he will kill me."

Raba replied, " Let him [*i.e.*, the prefect] kill you, but do not
commit murder. Why should you think that your blood is
redder than his? Perhaps his is redder than yours."
— *from Montefiore and Loewe, A Rabbinic Anthology*

This story preaches the noblest form of civil disobedience. One
can only assume that Ghandi and Martin Luther King would have
given the same advice.

Outwitting the Oppressor

Beruriah was the daughter of the martyred Hananiah ben
Teradyon. One day she said to Meir, her husband, "It's a most
terrible thing that my sister has been sent off by the Romans
to a house of prostitution; please see what you can do."

So Meir got together as much money as he could and went off
to find the place. At length he found it and he said, "If nothing
has happened to her yet, may a miracle take place so that she
be saved." Then he disguised himself as a Roman cavalry
officer and went in. He saw his sister-in-law and said to her
"Come sleep with me." But she made an excuse that it was
her menstruation period. "Then I will wait until you are well,"
he said. "Why wait?" she asked. "There are many prettier
women here." Meir soon learned the she had the same conversation with every man who approached her.

He then went to the guard and said to him, "Let me take her
away." The man replied, "I am scared." Meir offered him all
the money that he had brought: "Here, take all this money.
Keep half of it for yourself and use the other half to pay off
anyone who gets too inquisitive."

In due course the Roman governor learned that the girl had been released, and the poor guard was condemned to die. They led him out to be hanged and they lifted him to the scaffold. Then the condemned man prayed, "May the God of Meir help me!" Hearing this, the Romans brought him down from the scaffold and asked him what it was all about. The man felt compelled to tell them all about Meir, and the Romans made a likeness of the rabbi and posted it on the gates of the city with a notice, "Wanted dead or alive! Anyone who sees this man is ordered to bring him in."

One day, some Roman soldiers caught sight of the rabbi and started to chase him. Meir ran away, and to throw off suspicion from himself he ran into a brothel. Others say that he ran into a place selling forbidden food. He put a finger into the forbidden dish and licked another finger. When the Romans saw that they said, "This cannot be Rabbi Meir, for the rabbi would never taste such food!" So Meir escaped and went to Babylon.

> — adapted from Bialik and Ravnitsky, Stories of the Sages,
> from Sefer Ha'aggadah, selected by Chaim Pearl

Rabbi Meir was a renowned Talmudic sage who lived in Judea during the second century C.E. Here, he uses guile, bribery and deception to rescue his sister-in-law and escape from the Romans. He hopes for a miracle and then makes one happen. That is the humanist message in this story. (For more about his wife, Beruriah, see "A Rabbinical Sage Learns the Law from His Wife," Chapter VII.)

⌘ ⌘ ⌘

Shah Abbas was a wise and just ruler who would often disguise himself as a dervish and slip out among his people to see how they lived. One evening he saw a light in a poor hut and went in. A Jew sat in front of a dish of simple food, singing praises and songs of thanksgiving to God.

"Is a guest welcome?" the Shah asked.

"A guest is a gift of God," replied the Jew. "I do not have much, but you are welcome to share it with me."

After they had finished eating, the Shah said to him, "What is your work?"

"I am a cobbler," he answered. All day long I walk about the streets of the city and mend shoes."

The next day the Shah issued a decree that cobblers could no longer mend shoes without a permit. When the Jew heard of the new law, he went to the well and drew water for people in exchange for a few pennies.

When the disguised Shah returned that evening, he found the Jew as usual, singing praises to God.

"What did you do today?" he asked him.

"When I left my house this morning, I learned that I could no longer mend shoes, so I drew water and thus earned enough to buy bread."

"And what if the Shah issued a decree banning the drawing of water tomorrow?"

"Blessed is God day after day," answered the Jew.

The next day, the Shah issued a decree banning the drawing of water. When the Jew learned of it, he went and cut wood for several people in exchange for a few pennies. That night when the Shah returned, he found the Jew eating and singing as usual.

"What did you do today?" he asked the Jew.

"I found that I could no longer draw water, so I cut wood."

"And what if the Shah should forbid the cutting of wood tomorrow?" asked the Shah.

"Blessed is God day after day," said the Jew.

The next day the Shah sent messengers throughout the city proclaiming that all woodcutters must report for guard duty at the palace. The Jew went and was given a sword and told where to stand guard. Since he could not earn money that day, he went in the evening to the storekeeper and exchanged the steel blade of his sword for food. Then he went home and fashioned a wooden blade and attached it to the hilt of the sword. He was still working on the blade when the disguised Shah arrived.

"What are you doing?" the Shah asked him.

"I had to guard the palace today, so I could not earn money to buy food," the Jew told him. "I gave my sword blade as a pledge to the storekeeper, and now I am making a wooden one to replace it."

"And what if they should check swords tomorrow?" asked the Shah.

"Blessed is God day after day," answered the Jew.

The next day the captain of the guard summoned the Jew and placed a prisoner in his charge. "This prisoner has been condemned to death," he told the Jew, "You must cut off his head."

"I cannot," answered the Jew. "I have never killed a man in my life."

"It is the Shah's order!" said the captain. "You must obey!"

The Jew grasped the hilt of the sword and cried aloud to the crowd gathered to witness the execution, "God of the Universe! You know that I am no murderer! If the man who stands before me deserves to die, let my sword be a sword of steel. But if he is innocent, I pray that You turn this steel blade into a blade of wood!"

And when he drew forth the blade — behold! It was made of wood. The people gasped in astonishment. Then they let the prisoner go free.

After this, Shah Abbas summoned the Jew to the palace, embraced him, and revealed his true identity. He made the Jew one of his chief counselors and cherished him as a friend all the rest of his life.

— from Ellen Frankel,
The Classic Tales, 4,000 Years of Jewish Lore

Although the poor Jew repeatedly invokes God's power, his survival is clearly due to his own ingenuity. He manages to save his own life, avoid committing murder, cause a prisoner to be set free and rise to a position of power, while at all times acting like a true *mentsh*.

⌘⌘⌘

There is a story of King Don Pedro II and the sage Nicolao de Valencia. Nicolao said "Sire, I have learned that it is your desire to go to war. Now why should my lord proceed against those foes who are abroad and leave those who are at home? For there are the Jews who hate us so much and in whose books it is written that they must not greet us peaceably." Then the king answered: "Have you actually heard this with you own ears?" And Nicolao answered: "I have heard this from one of them who has come to our faith." "He," said the king, "is not worthy of belief, for one who changes his faith will find it easy to change the facts. And furthermore, hate based on religion is only doubtful hate, for it aims only to show his love of his new faith." But Nicolao answered: "All I am concerned for is their arrogance, for to your very face, sire, they will say that your faith is false!"

"Let us summon one of the wise Jews and ask him," said the king. When he appeared before him, the king ordered him to declare which of the two faiths was better, the faith of Jesus or the Jewish faith. The Jewish sage replied: "My faith is better for me, since I am what I am, for I was a slave in Egypt and God brought me forth from there, but your faith is better for you because of its constant and prolonged authority and duration."

"I ask you," said the king, "about the faiths in themselves and as such, not with respect to their followers." To this the Jew answered: "If it seems fit to you, your majesty, I shall answer you after three days of consideration." And the king said: "Be it so."

When the three days were over, the Jew came looking very grieved and disturbed. "Why do you look so downcast?" asked the king; and the Jew answered: "Because I was cursed today and groundlessly so, and I beseech you, your majesty, to take up my suit. This is what happened: About a month ago, my neighbor went on a long journey but left two precious stones for his two sons. Now the two brothers have come to me and requested me to tell them what the singular character of each stone is and the difference between them. 'Who knew that better than your father?' I said to them. 'There is no greater expert than he in all that concerns precious stones and the art of cutting them and not for nothing is he known to be a lapidary. Send for him and let him tell you the truth!' And because I gave them that reply, they cursed me and beat me."

"Why," exclaimed the king, "they cursed you without cause, and they deserve to be punished!"

Then the wise man answered: "Your majesty, let your own ears hearken to the words you uttered! Consider, Esau and Jacob were brothers and each one of them was given a certain jewel, and now your majesty asks which of them is better? Let the king send a messenger to our Father in heaven, for He is the great lapidary, and He will tell you the difference between the stones!"

"Do you see, Nicolao," exclaimed the king, "the wisdom of the Jews? This sage is indeed worthy of honor and gifts. As for you, you deserve to be punished for uttering falsehood about the Jewish community."
> *— from Mimekor Israel, Selected Classical Jewish Folktales,*
> *collected by Micha Joseph bin Gurion*

This story, known as "The Parable of the Precious Stones," is attributed to Solomon ibn Verga (1460-1554), a leader of the Spanish Jewish community who was expelled from Spain in 1492. He fled first to Portugal, where he was compelled to convert to Christianity, and then left for Turkey, where he returned to Judaism. He was a religious skeptic, a humanist thinker and a historian. Despite his experience with Christian persecution, he believed in religious tolerance. Although this story shows how Jews developed a keen intelligence in order to cope with precarious circumstances, it also expresses Solomon ibn Verga's sincere belief that Christianity and Judaism were equally deserving of respect.

⌘⌘⌘

A king had a counselor, a converted Jew, who hated the Jews
and looked for every chance to harm them. Once he appeared
before the king and said to him, "Your Majesty, I want you to
know that the Jews are sorcerers and can work miracles. In
fact, Moses, the miracle worker who took them out of Egypt,
is still living among them. They just keep it a secret."

And so the king gave the Jews three days in which to produce
Moses or perish.

The Jews called a fast and sat in the synagogue, praying and
weeping. A day went by and then a second and they could
think of no way to save themselves. As they were on their
way to synagogue on the morning of the third day, they spied
a Jew eating and drinking unconcernedly, as if the wicked
fellow had no God in his heart.

"Why are you eating?" they asked him.

"Why aren't you?" he asked back. And when told the reason,
he exclaimed, "And to think I didn't know!" Then he said,
"Now that you mention it, why don't you tell the king that I
am Moses? If he believes me, so much the better – and if he
doesn't, the most he can do is kill me, and you say he'll kill us
all anyway."

So the man dressed up in flowing robes of the sort that were
worn long ago, took a long stick, appeared before the king,
and announced, "I'm Moses!" The king called for his counselor to ask if this really was so. The counselor tried not to laugh
and said, "Let your majesty test the man and we'll see."

"What miracles can you work for me, Moses?" asked the
king.

"Your Majesty," said the man, "I'm prepared to work a miracle for you such as you've never seen before. Bring me a tub filled with boiling oil and throw your counselor in it, and I'll not only pull him out unharmed, I promise he'll be twenty years younger!"

Hearing this, the counselor turned pale. "Your Majesty," he said, his knees shaking, "there's really no need for such a test. It's clear as day that this man is really Moses."

And so the king sent the man home with great honor, and there was merriment and joy among the Jews.
— *from Jewish Folktales, selected and retold by Pinhas Sadeh*

Notice how the Jew who saves the day is the one who sees no need for prayer, weeping or fasting. His ability comes from his own intelligence and strength of character.

The Courage to Criticize

One day Rabbi Judah, Rabbi Jose and Rabbi Simeon were discussing the political situation. Judah ben Gerim was listening to the conversation. When the matter of the Roman rulers came up, Rabbi Judah praised them and said, "These people have done some really good things. Look, they built markets and bridges and public bathing places."

Rabbi Simeon disputed this and said, "Whatever they have done they have done for their own nefarious purposes. The markets they established in order to set up brothels, the public bathing places for their own pleasure and the bridges so that their soldiers can get around more quickly to collect the taxes." Rabbi Jose was quiet during that part of the discussion. However, Judah ben Gerim reported the conversation to the governor. As a result, Rabbi Judah who had praised the Romans was rewarded. Rabbi Jose who kept silent was exiled

Rabbi Simeon who was so outspoken in his criticism was
sentenced to death.

*— from Bialik and Ravnitsky, Stories of the Sages,
from Sefer Ha'aggadah, selected by Chaim Pearl*

Simeon Bar Yochai, one of the second century rabbis featured in
this story, escaped from the Romans by hiding in a cave for many
years. There is another story about that experience in Chapter V,
"Life Must Go On," that shows the negative side to his militancy.

Korah: Demagogue or Dissident?

Korah is one of the most despised figures in the Torah because
he incited the Hebrews in the desert to rebel against Moses. However, from the Jewish secular humanist perspective, there is considerable merit in Korah's criticisms of Moses' authoritarian rule
and irrational rituals, the privileges of the priesthood and the oppressive burdens placed on the people by religious law. It is a
tribute to the open-mindedness of Jewish folklore that it gives Korah
an opportunity to have his say.

Korah and his people exclaimed: "Moses is king, his brother
did he appoint as high priest, his nephews as heads of the
priests, he allots to the priests the *heave* offering [a
dough-offering and monetary contribution] and many other
tributes."

Then he tried to make Moses appear ridiculous in the eyes of
the people. Shortly before this Moses had read to the people
the law of the fringes in the borders of their garments [*tsitsis*].
Korah now had garments of purple made for the two hundred
fifty men that followed him. Arrayed thus, Korah and his
company appeared before Moses and asked him if they were
required to attach fringes to the corners of these garments.
Moses answered, "Yes." Korah then began this argument.
"If," said he, "one fringe of purple suffices to fulfill the
commandment, should not a whole garment of purple answer

the requirement of the law, even if there is no special fringe of purple in the corners?

He continued to lay before Moses similar artful questions: "Must a *mezuza* be attached to the door post of a house filled with sacred books?" Moses answered, "Yes." Then Korah said: the two hundred and seventy sections of the Torah are not sufficient, whereas the two sections attached to the door post suffice!

Korah put still another question: "If upon a man's skin there shows a bright spot, is he clean or unclean?" Moses: "Unclean." "And," continued Korah, "if the spot spreads and covers all the skin of him, is he then clean or unclean?" Moses: "Clean." "Laws so irrational," said Korah, "cannot possibly trace their origin from God. The Torah that you teach to Israel is not therefore God's work, but your work, hence you are no prophet and Aaron is no high priest!"

Then Korah incited the people to rebellion against Moses, and particularly against the tributes the priests imposed on the people. That the people might now be in a position to form a proper conception of the oppressive burden of these tasks, Korah told them the following tale: "There lived in my vicinity a widow with two daughters, who owned for their support a field whose yield was just sufficient for them to keep body and soul together. When this woman set out to plow her field, Moses appeared and said: 'You shall not plow with an ox and an ass together.' When she began to sow, Moses appeared and said: 'You shall not sow with mixed seeds.' When the first crops showed in the poor widow's field, Moses appeared and told her to bring it to the priests, since they are due 'the first of all the fruit of the earth,' and when at length the time came for her to harvest, Moses appeared and ordered her not wholly to reap the corners of the field, nor to gather the gleanings of the harvest, but to leave them for the poor. When she had

done all that Moses had bidden her, and was about to thrash
the grain, Moses appeared once more, and said: 'Give me the
heave offering, the first and the second tithes to the priests.'

"When at last the poor woman became aware that she could
not possibly survive from the yield of the field after the
deduction of all the tributes that Moses had imposed upon her,
she sold the field and with the proceeds purchased lambs, in
the hope that she might now have the benefit of the wool as
well as of the offspring. She was, however, mistaken. When
the first lambs were born, Aaron appeared and demanded it,
for the firstborns belong to the priest. At the shearing time,
Aaron reappeared and demanded 'the first of the fleece of the
sheep,' which, according to Moses' law, was his. But not
content with this, he reappeared later and demanded one sheep
out of every ten as a tithe.

"This, however, was too much for the long-suffering woman,
and she slaughtered the sheep, supposing that she might now
feel herself secure. But this was not to be! Aaron appeared,
and, basing his claim on the Torah, demanding the shoulder,
the two cheeks, and the maw. 'Alas!' exclaimed the woman,
'The slaughtering of the sheep did not deliver me out of your
hands! Let the meat then be consecrated to the sanctuary.'
Aaron said, 'Everything devoted in Israel is mine.' He departed, taking with him the meat of the sheep and leaving
behind the widow and her daughters weeping bitterly. Such
men," said Korah, concluding his tale, "are Moses and Aaron,
who pass their cruel measures as Divine laws."
                                — *adapted from Louis Ginzberg, Legends of the Bible*

In the Torah (*Num. 26:11*), Korah and more than two hundred fifty
of his followers were wiped out by God for defying Moses. However, his sons survived and their descendants became musicians
and poets in the First Temple.

Defying Illegitimate Authority

At the Seder on the night of Passover, Rabbi Mendel of
Rymanov liked to tell the following story after the song about
"only one kid" [*Chad Gadya*]:

A peasant stood in the marketplace and offered a calf for sale.
Along came the lord of the manor and asked: "What do you
want for that dog?" Said the peasant: "That's a calf and not a
dog." Each insisted that he was right and so they wrangled for
a while, until the lord gave the peasant a box on the ear,
saying: "Here's something to help you remember that when
the lord says it's a dog, it is a dog." The peasant replied: "I
shall remember."

Some time later, a friend of the peasant came running into the
village which adjoined the manor. He was all out of breath
and shouted for the firemen. It seemed that where he lived,
quite a distance away, the community threshing barn and the
house of the lord had caught fire. The entire squad of firemen
set out and took all their equipment with them. In the meantime, the peasant set fire to the manor and burned it down.

A few weeks later, when he heard that the lord was going to
rebuild his house, he disguised himself, pretending to be an
architect and told the lord he would draw up a plan. This at
once he proceeded to do, for he was a clever peasant. They sat
over the plan, calculated the amount of wood necessary for the
building, and decided to go into the forest that belonged to the
lord to measure the circumference of the trees that were
suitable for lumber.

When they reached the forest, the peasant was contemptuous
of the trees standing at the edge. There were better trees
farther along, said the lord. They walked on, keeping a sharp
lookout, until they were right in the middle of the forest.
There the architect stopped and pointed enthusiastically to a

giant of a tree, saying it was so many feet around and would make splendid planks.

Then the lord went up to the tree and put his arms around the trunk. "Just as I figured!" he cried. The peasant pulled out his measuring cord, tied the lord to the trunk by his arms and legs, gave him a sound drubbing and said: "This is the first re- minder, so that you'll know when a peasant says it's a calf, it is a calf and not a dog." Then he went his way, but the lord howled for hours until someone happened along and cut his bonds.

When the lord got home he felt ill and went to bed. He grew worse from day to day and had doctor after doctor call, but none of them could give him any relief. At that time a rumor spread through the neighboring town that a great miracle- healer would stop there for a day in the course of his travels and would heal all the sick who came to consult him.

Soon after, the peasant, disguised as a doctor, arrived in town, and gave out very good advice, for he was a clever peasant. The lord, who had heard of him, had him summoned to his bedside and promised to pay him whatever he asked if he would cure him.

The doctor came, took one look at the patient, and said to the persons around him: "You must leave me alone with him and not disturb me in my rather severe but infallible cure – not even if he should scream." As soon as they were gone, he bolted the door and gave the lord another first-rate drubbing.

Those who stood outside heard the pitiful shrieks and said: "There is a real fellow for you! He is doing a thorough job." But the peasant was saying to the lord: "This is a second reminder, so you'll be sure to know once and for all: When a peasant says it's a calf, it *is* a calf and not a dog." Then he went off with such ease and self-confidence that no one even thought of stopping him.

When the lord recovered from his illness and his bruises, he set out to find the peasant, but he did not succeed, for the latter had not only dyed his skin and changed the cut of his hair, but had also assumed manners and gestures that were so different that he was quite unrecognizable. Early in the morning on the next market day, he saw the lord sitting in his coach close to the marketplace which was still almost empty, peering in all directions. The peasant turned to an acquaintance of his who had come with his horse and had the reputation of being a good rider, and said: "Do you want to do me a favor, friend?" "Surely," said the other, "if it isn't anything too difficult."

"All you have to do," answered the peasant, "is to ride up to that gentleman in the coach, bend down and whisper to him: 'If a peasant says it's a calf, it *is* a calf.' Then ride off as fast as you can and don't stop until you have left those who pursue you far behind. After that, meet me at the inn — you know which — and I'll have them serve you the best plum brandy ever."

His friend did as he had been told. When the lord heard his words, he started up, for he was sure the man he had been looking for was there in front of him. He shouted to his coachman and servant to unhitch the horses and make after the fellow. They mounted the horses and galloped off.

When the peasant saw the lord alone in his coach, he went up to him, boxed his ears soundly and said: "This is the third reminder, and now I guess you have learned that when a peasant says it's a calf, it is a calf and not a dog." Then he went off to the inn.

And the calf — so Rabbi Mendel ended his tale at every Seder — the calf remained a calf and never became a dog.

And when the children asked: "And what was the name of the clever peasant? Rabbi Mendel answered, "Michael" [the most important angel].

When they asked: "What was the name of the bad lord?" he said: "Sammael" [Satan].

And when they asked: "What was the name of the calf that never became a dog?" he replied: That is the well-known calf, Israel."
— *from Martin Buber, Tales of the Hasidim: The Later Masters*

This story is interesting for a number of reasons. It casts a gentile peasant as the hero, depicts the lord as an arrogant tyrant and condones the use of violence. Yes, the revenge part is a bit over-done, but the message of this parable is clear: Despite efforts to eradicate us and our culture, *am yisrael chai* (the people of Israel live!)

⌘⌘⌘

It happened in a Russian town in the days of the Czar. A party of convicts was being led to prison. It included three Jews. As they shuffled through the streets loaded with chains, some Jewish women began to commiserate loudly with them.

"Why are they taking you?" they mournfully asked one Jewish convict.

"It's on account of my residence permit," he answered with a sigh.

Hearing this, the women wailed, "*Oy, nebich!* (alas!) What a wrong! and just for a mere residence permit!

"And why are they punishing you?" they asked the second Jew.

"It's because I didn't want to be a soldier in the army of that Haman, Czar Nicolai!"

"*Oy, nebich!*" wailed the women even more loudly. "What a shame--what cruelty! And just because he didn't wish to serve that dog of dogs, that antisemite!"

Then the third Jewish convict, a muscular fellow with squint eyes and a scar on his face, passed by.

"Tell us, why are they taking you?" the women inquired.

"Who, me?" he asked piteously. "I am *nebich a gonif* (a thief)."

— *from Ausubel, A Treasury of Jewish Folklore*

Such is the *koved* (honor) attached to being the victim of Czarist persecution, that the common criminal feels compelled to apologize to the Jewish women for being the only one of the three Jewish prisoners who arguably deserves his punishment.

⌘⌘⌘

To a rabbinical school in Old Russia, the military came in search of recruits. The entire student body was drafted.

In camp, the students amazed their new masters by their marksmanship on the rifle range. Accordingly, when war broke out, the yeshiva youths were ordered en masse into the front lines.

Shortly after the contingent arrived an attack began. Far in the distance, in No Man's Land, an advancing horde of Germans appeared. The Czarist officers called out, "Ready ... aim ... fire!"

But no fire was forthcoming.

"Fire!" yelled the officers. "Didn't you hear? Fire, you idiots, fire!"

Still nothing happened.

Beside himself with rage, the commanding officer demanded, "Why don't you fire?"

One of the youths mildly answered, "Can't you see ... there are people in the way. Somebody might get hurt!"
— *from Ausubel, A Treasury of Jewish Folklore*

Of course, not shooting also poses a serious problem if the other side refuses to play by the same rules, but the *yeshiva bokhers'* (boys') refusal to obey orders is still admirable. On one level, it reflects a commitment to nonviolence, but it also raises the question of whether any oppressed people should pick up the gun to defend their oppressors.

How to Administer Justice

During his march to conquer the world, Alexander [the Great], the Macedonian, came to a people in Africa who dwelt in a remote and secluded corner in peaceful huts and knew neither war nor conqueror.

They led him to the hut of their chief, who received him hospitably. "For what reason, then, art thou come amongst us?" asked the chief.

"To become acquainted with your manners and customs," answered Alexander.

"So be it," rejoined the other. "Sojourn among us as long as it pleaseth thee."

At the close of this conversation, two citizens entered into their court of justice.

The plaintiff said: "I bought of this man a piece of land, and as I was making a deep drain through it, I found a treasure. This is not mine, for I only bargained for the land, and not for any treasure that might be concealed beneath it; and yet the former owner of the land will not receive it."

The defendant answered: "I hope I have a conscience, as well as my fellow-citizen. I sold him the land with all its contingent, as well as existing advantages, and consequently the treasure inclusively."

The chief, who was at the same time their supreme judge, recapitulated their words, in order that the parties might see whether or not he understood them aright. Then, after some reflection, he said, "Thou hast a son, friend, I believe?"

"Yes."

"And thou," addressing the other, "a daughter?"

"Yes."

"Well, then, let thy son marry *thy* daughter, and bestow the treasure on the young couple for a marriage portion."

Alexander seemed surprised and perplexed.

"You think my sentence unjust?" the chief asked him.

"Oh no!" replied Alexander. "But it astonished me."

"And how then", rejoined the chief, "would the case have been decided in your country?"

"To confess the truth," said Alexander, "we should have taken both parties into custody and have seized the treasure for the king's use."

"For the king's use!" exclaimed the chief. "Does the sun shine on your country?"

"Oh yes!"

"Does it rain there?"

"Assuredly."

"Wonderful! But are there tame animals in the country, that live on the grass and green herbs?"

"Very many and of many kinds."

"Aye, that must then be the cause," said the chief. "For the sake of those innocent animals the all-gracious Being continues to let the sun shine and the rain drop down on your own country, since its inhabitants are unworthy of such blessings."
— *from Ausubel, A Treasury of Jewish Folklore*

This story, taken from the *Aggada*, appears in numerous collections. It shows that Jewish folklore recognized that "backward" people could be more advanced than "civilized" ones when it comes to dealing justly with their fellow human beings. Unfortunately, our greatest medieval scholar, Maimonides, believed that Black Africans ("Kushites") and Mongols ("distant tribes of 'Turks'") were mentally inferior. Stories like this explain why Secular Humanistic Jews value the aggadic over the halakhic tradition.

Is There a Right Choice?

Ulla Bar Hoshab fled and went into hiding. He had disobeyed the Queen; therefore, he feared her vengeance. For this reason she condemned him to death.

He finally found asylum with Rabbi Joshua ben Levi in the town of Ludd. But the Queen's spies discovered his hiding place. They surrounded the house and said to the Jews, "If you do not deliver to us this man we will slaughter all the Jews in your town."

Then Rabbi Joshua ben Levi said to Ulla bar Koshab, "I beg you to forgive me if I deliver you to the Queen's servants. Far better that a single person should suffer than that an entire populace should be slaughtered."

Then he went and delivered Ulla to the Queen's spies.

Now in the past, the Prophet Elijah had often miraculously revealed himself to Rabbi Joshua ben Levi. But after Rabbi Joshua delivered Ulla to the Queen's spies, Elijah ceased his visits. Grieved over his continued absence, Rabbi Joshua fasted for thirty days. Then Elijah came again.

"Why did you desert me?" asked Rabbi Joshua.

"What else did you expect?" cried Elijah, "Should I have anything to do with a man who delivers an innocent fellow-Jew into the hands of the heathen?"

"I have only done as the law bids me," Rabbi Joshua said, in justification. "The Mishna teaches us that, when the heathen demand that a single Jew be delivered to them with the threat of killing all other Jews if this be not done, then it is right to sacrifice the individual for the entire community."

"The law is as you say," replied Elijah sternly, "but under no circumstances should you have acted as you did. Better that all should perish than that Jews, with their own hands, should deliver a brother to be murdered by the enemy."
                              — *from Ausubel, A Treasury of Jewish Folklore*

This is actually a point of controversy according to Jewish law, with arguments on both sides. The next story deals with the same issue.

⌘⌘⌘

A woodsman went into the forest to ask the trees to give him wood for an ax. It seemed so modest a request that the principal trees at once agreed to it, and it was settled among them that the plain, unpretentious ash should furnish what was wanted.

No sooner had the woodsman fitted the staff to his purpose than he began laying about him on all sides, felling the noblest trees in the forest. The oak whispered to the cedar: "Our first concession has lost us all. If we had not sacrificed our humblest neighbor, we ourselves might have stood for ages."
—*from William B. Silverman,*
The Sages Speak: Rabbinical Wisdom and Jewish Values

This was a dilemma that plagued the Judenrat (Jewish Councils) set up by the Nazis. Most thought they could placate the Nazis by turning over some of their own and ended up being accessories to mass murder.

The Story of the Golem: the Defender of the Jews

In the city of Worms, there dwelt a certain great and saintly man named Rabbi Bezalel unto whom a son was born on Passover eve in the middle of the Seder ceremony. This befell in the year five thousand two hundred and seventy-three of the Creation (1513), when Israel was being grievously persecuted by the Christian peoples. For they charged them with requiring Christian blood for the Passover Festival in order to mix it in their unleavened bread. Now the very birth of Rabbi Bezalel's son brought about deliverance. For when his mother felt the birth pangs and the members of the household hurried into the street in order to fetch a midwife, they found people

bearing a dead Christian child in a sack in order to bring a
false charge against the Jews. And Rabbi Bezalel his father
prophesied about his son: "He will console us and deliver us
from the blood libel."

The child grew up into a great scholar and was also very wise,
knowing all the sciences and all languages. He became a rabbi
in the city of Posen and from there was appointed rabbi and
head of the court in the holy congregation of Prague in the
year five thousand three hundred and thirty-two of the Creation (1571/72). When he was welcomed as rabbi it was a
time of distress for the Jews on account of the blood charge,
from which they suffered a great deal. Much blood of Jewish
souls, who were completely innocent, was groundlessly shed,
like water, on account of that despicable charge.

So the rabbi asked a question of the heavens in a dream. He
asked by what power he could withstand the priests who were
opposed to the Jews. The answer that reached him followed
the letters of the Hebrew alphabet: And Be Creating, Dedicate
Earth Fittingly, Golem Handles Israel's Jew-Hating
Knife-Bearers.

Now the sage decided that these ten words contained various
combinations of divine names by the power of which it would
be possible to fashion a living golem from earthy matter. So
he secretly summoned both his son-in-law and his great
disciple, Rabbi Jacob Sasson, and showed them the response
from heaven, which he had obtained as answer to his dream
query. And he entrusted them both with the secret regarding
the creation of the Golem from clay and earth of the ground.

The three of them left the city of Prague for the river. There
they searched along the riverbank until they found a spot
containing clay and mud, and from it they fashioned the shape

of a man three ells long, and they drew a face in it and made
him hands and feet, and when they had finished, this was like
a man lying on his back. Then the three of them stood at the
Golem's feet facing his face, and the rabbi ordered his
son-in-law to make a circuit of the Golem seven times, pro-
ceeding from the right and going around as far as the golem's
head, and from the head to the feet on the left. And he entrusted him with combinations of letters to be uttered as he
made the circuit. This he did seven times. When the circuits
were completed, the body of the Golem had grown as red as
glowing coals.

The rabbi instructed his disciple to make seven such circuits
likewise, and entrusted him with other permutations and
combinations of letters. The disciple did what his master
required and when he completed his circuits, the fire died
down, for water reached the body and vapor began to rise
from it, nails sprouted at the fingertips, and he likewise
became as hairy as a thirty-year-old man. Then the rabbi
likewise made seven circuits around the Golem and after he
had completed them, the three of them together recited the
verse that is in the Book of Genesis: "And He breathed the
spirit of life into his nostrils, and man became a living creature" (2:7).

When they had finished reciting this verse, the Golem opened
his eyes and stared at the rabbi and his disciples like a man in
confusion. Then the rabbi called him in a commanding voice:
"Rise to your feet!" And the Golem rose to his feet. They clad
him in garments which they had taken with them, such garments as were suited to a court attendant. And they also put
boots on his feet.

Then the rabbi said to the Golem: "Know that we have created
you of earth from the ground in order that you should guard
the Jews from all evil and distress that they suffer at the hands

of their foes and traducers. Your name will be Joseph. You will live with me and dwell in the courtyard of my court. You will work as a bailiff, and you will obey my orders in all that I command you, even if it is to enter the fire or drown in the great waters or leap from the tower, until you have performed my command in its entirety and done whatever I have sent you to do!"

The Golem always sat in a corner of the courtroom beside the table, leaning his head on his two hands like a true golem that has no wisdom or understanding. He neither thought nor was concerned with any matter in the world. The rabbi said about him that if he were to walk through fire he would not be scorched, and river currents would not sweep him away, nor would the sword slay him.

The rabbi made use of the Golem only to deliver Israel from trouble and distress. Most of all he used him in order to combat the blood charge which, as already remarked, was exceedingly widespread, so that the Jewish residents of the city of Prague and the vicinity suffered greatly from it.

During the whole month before Passover he used to patrol the streets of the Jewish quarter at night by order of the rabbi. If he saw any man carrying a burden on his shoulder or dragging some burden in a cart, he would run to him and inspect what he was carrying or dragging. If he saw that this was a dead child that they wished to fling into the street of the Jews, he would seize the man and the corpse and bind them together with a rope he wore corded around him and would drag them by force to the council house, where the chief constable and city watch were to be found; and there the man would be imprisoned and judged as a criminal.

The might of the Golem was above the natural, and he did a great deal as long as he existed.

After the law that no trials on the blood charge would be heard any more was published and the land grew quiet, the rabbi made an end of the Golem. He commanded his disciples to make a circuit around him seven times by night and to repeat the permutations and combinations of letters which they had uttered when he was fashioned, but in the opposite order. When the seventh circuit was completed, the Golem remained lying like a piece of hardened clay without any spirit of life.

They removed his garments, wrapped him up in two old prayer shawls, and concealed him under a pile of tattered books in the rabbi's attic.

— adapted from Mimekor Israel,
Selected Classical Jewish Folktales,
collected by Micha Joseph bin Gurion

The rabbi depicted in this story is meant to be Judah Loew ben Bezalel a.k.a. "the Maharal," who lived in Prague, 1520-1609. He may not have created a superhuman creature to protect the Jews of Prague from the ritual murder accusation, but he did demand "justice for my oppressed brothers" in confronting the Dominican monk Thaddeus who was inciting Christian mobs against Jews. In a public debate, he cited the Bible to prove that Jewish law forbade the consumption of blood and the Talmud to prove that even the shedding of blood was forbidden.

Another version of this famous story had a role in inspiring Mary Shelley's *Frankenstein*: The Golem goes berserk, indiscriminately killing Gentiles until the Maharal destroys it.

Chapter III.
Mentshlekhkayt
(Human Decency)

If I am not for myself, who will be? But if I am for myself only, what am I? And if not now, when?

— Hillel, from Pirke Avot

He whose wisdom exceeds his good deeds; to what can he be compared? To a tree with many branches and few roots; and the wind comes and uproots it. ... But he whose good deeds exceed his wisdom; to what can he be compared? To a tree with few branches and many roots, so that even if the strongest winds would blow, it will not move. As it is written (Jeremiah 17:8): And he shall be like a tree planted by the waters, that spreads its roots by a stream. It does not suffer from the heat and its leaves are always green. It can survive a drought, and continues to bear fruit.

— Rabbi Elazar ben Azaryah, from Pirke Avot

Rabban Yohanan asked his disciples to reflect on the highest good that a person should strive to attain. Rabbi Eliezer said generosity; Rabbi Joshua said friendship; Rabbi Yose said concern for one's neighbor; Rabbi Simeon said considering the consequences of one's actions; Rabbi Elazar said a kind heart. Rabban

*Yohanan replied, "I prefer the opinion of Rabbi Elazar
because your views are embodied in his."*
                                              — Pirke Avot

*In a place where there are no men [translation: decent
human beings], you must strive to be a man.*
                                  — adapted from Hillel, Pirke Avot

⌘⌘⌘

A rich but stingy man once came to his rabbi to ask for his
blessing. The rabbi suddenly arose, took him by the hand, and
led him to the window looking out on the street.

"Tell me, what do you see?" asked the rabbi.

"I see people," answered the puzzled rich man.

Then the rabbi drew him before a mirror.

"What do you see now?" he asked him again.

"I see myself," answered the man, bewildered.

"Now, my son, let me explain to you the meaning of my two
questions. The window is made of glass, as is also the mirror.
Only the glass of the mirror has a veneer of silver on it. When
you look through plain glass you see people. But no sooner do
you cover it with silver, then you stop seeing others and see
only yourself."
                          — from Ausubel, A Treasury of Jewish Folklore

⌘⌘⌘

The Primacy of Ethical Behavior
Gaining Entrance to Heaven

When man appears before the Throne of Judgment, the first question he is asked is not: "Did you believe in God?" or "Did you pray and observe the rituals?" He is asked: "Have you dealt honorably and faithfully in all your dealings with your fellow man?" *(Talmud, Shabbat 31a).*
> — *from Newman and Spitz, The Talmudic Anthology*

A classic and succinct statement of the humanist ideal.

⌘⌘⌘

Solomon Ben Isaac, known as Rashi, was the greatest Jewish scholar of his generation (1040-1105 C.E.). When he reached his sixtieth birthday, he wished to know who would be his companion in Paradise.

"Surely my companion will be a righteous and learned man!" thought Rashi.

That night God revealed to him in a dream that his future companion would be Don Abraham Gerson, the *Tsaddik* (the Righteous), who lived in Barcelona.

"Surely this Don Abraham is an old man with white hair and a long, white beard," thought Rashi when he awoke the next morning, "a pious man whose wrinkled face is pale from years of study but whose eyes are still clear and filled with wisdom."

Eagerly he prepared himself for a long journey and then set off for Spain. When he reached Barcelona, he went straight to the synagogue.

"Where might I find *Abraham*, the Tsaddik?" he asked.

They all shook their heads. No one by that name lived in Barcelona. Disappointed, Rashi turned to go. Then he had an idea.

"Have you by any chance heard of Abraham Gerson?"

"Abraham Gerson!" they cried. "But he is an apostate! He eats food prepared by Gentiles, violates the Sabbath and never sets foot in the synagogue. What do you want with him?"

Rashi was very surprised to hear these things about his future companion in Paradise, but he thought, "Perhaps I have been sent to bring him back to the right path."

So he went to Abraham Gerson's house. How surprised he was to find himself standing before a magnificent mansion! A servant ushered him inside, where he saw broad marble staircases, beautiful gardens and servants scurrying to and fro in gold livery.

"There must be some mistake," thought Rashi. "What sins have I committed to merit such an unholy companion in the World to Come?"

Just then Don Abraham Gerson appeared. He was a young man of about thirty, very handsome and proud.

"I am Rabbi Solomon ben Isaac," declared Rashi. "I come in the name of God!"

"I am sure that you do," answered Don Abraham, smiling. "So you are the famous Rashi! Your name has reached us even here in Spain. Let us be friends. I invite you to come to my wedding tomorrow."

"Is it a Gentile woman you are marrying?" asked Rashi.

"No."

"Surely a wealthy woman then?" said Rashi.

"No," answered Don Abraham.

Just then a servant interrupted their conversation. "There is a poor woman outside who wishes to be admitted."

"Let her wait," replied Don Abraham.

"How can you be so heartless?" protested Rashi. "Perhaps she is in dire need."

So they went to the woman and asked her what she wanted.

"I do not come to beg for bread," she told them, "for Don Abraham has already distributed alms to the poor in honor of his wedding tomorrow."

"What then do you want of me?" asked Don Abraham, growing impatient.

"I have come to you for advice," she said. "I am a poor woman, a widow with four children. Three of my children are too young to work for wages, so my oldest son must support us all. Now he is dangerously ill, and I fear we will be left without anyone to support us."

"I will be glad to send my own physician to tend your son," offered Don Abraham.

"No, it is not disease that has stricken my son but disappointed love. He had hoped to marry a poor girl whom he loves dearly, but the girl's parents are forcing her to marry a rich man against her will."

"Why are you telling me all this?" asked Don Abraham.

"Because you are that rich man!" cried the mother, pointing an accusing finger at the startled man.

"What is your son's name?" asked Don Abraham.

"Don Abraham ben Manuel," she replied.

"You and your family are invited to my wedding tomorrow," said Don Abraham. Then without another word, he turned and walked away.

Rashi ran after him. "Don Abraham!" he cried. "Do not be overly distressed by this woman's words. People cannot die of love. The young man will soon recover."

"No," answered Don Abraham. "I fear he will not."

"In time he will find another woman, and this one will become only a fond memory."

"No," said Don Abraham again. "There is only one sun in heaven. Take it away and all is dark. Life without love is nothing."

"Nonsense!" cried Rashi. "Time heals all wounds. But you are right to be concerned about the family. Until the son recovers, they are in need of help."

"Indeed they are, Rabbi," said Don Abraham, and his voice carried an infinite sadness. Then his face brightened and he said, "Remember to come to my wedding tomorrow!"

Bidding him goodbye, Rashi departed and returned the next day.

When he entered Don Abraham's house, he found the marble pavement strewn with flowers, the courtyard filled with many guests wearing rich, brightly colored clothes and a beautiful wedding canopy set up in the center. In one corner huddled the poor widow and her four children, her eldest son leaning weakly upon her arm. A hush suddenly fell over the crowd as the veiled bride was led to the canopy to stand beside Don Abraham. Then the marriage contract was read.

"There has been a terrible mistake!" announced Don Abraham at the conclusion of the reading. "The bridegroom's name is not Abraham Gerson but Abraham ben Manuel. I have only been the matchmaker in this marriage. Tomorrow I am going abroad to conduct some business. I leave Don Abraham ben Manual in charge of my affairs while I am gone." He paused, and Rashi saw that his eyes were filled with tears. Then he smiled through the tears. "Come here, young man," he beckoned to the pale young man in the corner. "I want to wish you and your new bride a long life and much happiness!"

As soon as the young man stood under the canopy, the rabbi concluded the ceremony, and then the musicians began to play. The newly married couple seemed not to hear a sound, so lost were they in each other's gaze.

Rashi now turned to Don Abraham and said, "You are indeed worthy to share my table in Paradise!" and he told Don Abraham about the dream sent to him by God.

Don Abraham smiled and said, " I am delighted to have such an excellent companion in the next world. For as you can see, I shall be coming alone."
—*from Frankel, The Classic Tales, 4000 Years of Jewish Lore*

This is one of a series of stories with the same message. A man who does not follow Jewish ritual or devote himself to religious study turns out to be a moral exemplar. Of course, neither the observant nor the secular Jew has a monopoly on morality, but it is clear from this story that eating unkosher food, not keeping the Sabbath and never attending synagogue does not disqualify a Jew from being a *mentsh* (a decent person) or even a *tsaddik* (a righteous person).

⌘⌘⌘

Rabbi Simeon once prayed to the Almighty to show him the place reserved for him in Paradise. God answered his prayer, and he found out that his neighbor in the World to Come would be a butcher. Hearing this, Rabbi Simeon was filled with amazement.

"How can that be?" he asked himself in vexation. "All the days and nights of my life I have devoted to the study of the Torah; all my efforts I have directed to the greater glory of God. Why, then, do I deserve the humiliation of being placed next to a common butcher in Paradise?"

Rabbi Simeon thought: "I will call on this butcher and find out what manner of a man he is."

He did so and learned that he was very rich. The butcher was hospitable, and Rabbi Simeon lived in his house for eight days. He was accorded all the honors due his illustrious rank.

One day Rabbi Simeon invited him for a walk in the fields. On the way he asked him, "Pray tell me, to what ends have you devoted your life?"

And the butcher replied, "I know I am a sinner. I've neglected to study the Torah and have bent all my thoughts to the affairs of my shop. At first I was poor, but in time I began to prosper.

However, in my good fortune I never forgot the needy. I distributed alms, and for every Sabbath I provided all the poor of the town, and even those of the surrounding towns, with goodly portions of meat."

Still Rabbi Simeon remained unconvinced. Was the giving of charity enough to place a common butcher on the same level with him, the Light of the Age?

"It seems to me you must have done something more meritorious than that!" he exclaimed.

"I really cannot think of anything," replied the butcher, "except one unusual thing that once happened to me.

"At the time I was the customs collector of this city. Whenever a ship arrived in the harbor, I would go aboard to examine the cargo and to collect the customs.

"Once a ship arrived and I went aboard. The captain said to me, 'I am carrying a valuable cargo in the hold of my ship. Possibly you might wish to buy it.'

"'Show it to me,' I replied.

"He then brought up on deck two hundred Jewish slaves in chains.

"'How much do you want for them?' I asked.

"'I want ten thousand gold pieces for them. If you won't buy them, I'll cast them all into the sea and let them drown.'

"I had compassion for my Jewish brothers. I bought them and led them ashore. I fed and clothed them and provided them with lodgings. Then I paired the marriageable youths and girls among them, provided dowries for them and married them off according to the Laws of Moses.

"Now it happened that among them was a beautiful girl. She awakened the deepest sympathy in me, so I gave her as a wife to my son.

"I had invited to the wedding feast all the people of my town, among them the Jewish slaves I had redeemed. But I noticed an extraordinary thing: amidst all the rejoicing a youth, one of the former slaves, sat alone and shed tears.

"'Why do you weep?' I asked him.

"But he did not answer.

"I then led him into a private room and this is what he told me:

"'On the very day that he and his comrades had been seized as slaves he was to have married the beautiful girl who had now become my son's wife.

"So I said to him, 'Renounce all thought of her and I will give you a large sum of money!'

"He answered, 'Far better than all the gold and silver in the world I would have for my wife this girl whom I love! But now, alas! It is too late! She is already married to your son!'

"When I heard these words and saw his grief I went to my son and told him of all this.

"'I will divorce her,' cried my son, 'so that she can marry the youth she loves.'

"And this he did. I gave her a dowry and she married the youth."

When Rabbi Simeon heard the butcher's words he exclaimed, "Praise be the Lord on High who has decreed that I shall sit next to you in Paradise!"
— from Ausubel, A Treasury of Jewish Folklore

By virtue of his good deeds, a simple butcher has the same claim to Paradise as a religious scholar. This is quite a lesson, considering the central role that rabbinic Judaism assigns to Torah study — and one that Secular Humanistic Jews can readily subscribe to.

⌘ ⌘ ⌘

Rabbi Joshua was very pious and learned in the Law. Once, in a dream, a voice spoke to him: "Rejoice, Joshua, because you and Nenes, the butcher, will sit side by side in Paradise and your reward will be the same."

When Rabbi Joshua awoke he cried, "Woe is me! Even since childhood I have devoted myself to the service of the Lord, studied the Torah without end and illuminated the minds of eighty disciples. Now see the reward I will be getting for all my good deeds! It seems I'm no better that Nenes, the butcher!"

He then sent for his disciples and said to them, "I will not enter the House of Study with you until I find Nenes the butcher and learn from him what it is that he has done to deserve being my companion in Paradise."

From town to town Rabbi Joshua went with his disciples in search of Nenes the butcher, but no one had ever heard of him. At last, after much wandering, they came to the village where Nenes lived. Rabbi Joshua then began to make inquiries about him.

"O, learned Rabbi!" the townsfolk asked him. "How is it that a man of your eminence should be asking after such an ignoramus and insignificant person?"

But Rabbi Joshua persisted: "Tell me what kind of man is he?"

"Don't ask us, Rabbi," they replied. "You'll see for yourself."

So they sent for the butcher, saying, "Rabbi Joshua is here and would like to see you." Nenes was astonished.

"Who am I," he exclaimed, "that a great man like Rabbi Joshua should wish to see me? I'm afraid you've come to make sport of me! I will not go with you!"

Chagrined, the townsfolk returned to Rabbi Joshua and said, "O, Light of Israel! Light of our eyes and crown of our head! Why have you sent us to such a boor? He has refused to come with us."

"I will not go from here," cried Rabbi Joshua, "until I have seen Nenes, the butcher! In fact, I will go to him myself."

When the butcher caught sight of Rabbi Joshua he became frightened. "O, Crown of Israel!" he exclaimed. "Why do you wish to see me?"

"I wish to put to you some questions," answered Rabbi Joshua. "Tell me, what good have you done in your life?"

"I am an ordinary butcher. I have a father and a mother who are old and weak. I've given up all my pleasures to attend to their needs. I wash and dress them and prepare their food with my own hands."

When Rabbi Joshua heard these words he bent down and kissed the butcher on the forehead, saying, "My son, blessed are you and blessed is your good fortune! How happy am I to have the distinction of being your companion in Paradise!"
— from Ausubel, A Treasury of Jewish Folklore

As we have seen, this is a recurring theme in Jewish folklore. The virtues of a scholar are no worthier than the good deeds of a simple decent person.

⌘⌘⌘

The gates of Paradise stood open and the procession of the souls of men reached to the Heavenly Tribunal.

First came a rabbi.

"I'm learned in the Law," he said. "Night and day have I pored over the Word of God. I therefore deserve a place in Paradise."

"Just a moment!" called out the Recording Angel. "First we must make an investigation. We've got to find out what was the motive for your study. Did you apply yourself to learning for its own sake? Was it for the sake of honor, or for mercenary reasons?"

Next came a saintly man.

"How I fasted in the life I left behind! I observed all the six hundred and thirteen religious duties scrupulously. I bathed several times a day, and I studied the mysteries of the Zohar ceaselessly."

"Just a moment!" cried the Recording Angel. "We first have to make our investigation about the purity of your intentions."

Then a tavern-keeper approached. He said simply, "My door was always open to the homeless and I fed whoever was in need and hungry."

"Open the Gates of Paradise!" cried the Recording Angel. "No investigation is needed."
                                    — from Ausubel, A Treasury of Jewish Folklore

And no further comment is required.

⌘⌘⌘

Once Rabbi Baroka walked through the crowded marketplace of his town and met Elijah, the wandering spirit of prophecy in Jewish lore. "Who of all this multitude has the best claim to heaven?" asked the rabbi. Elijah pointed out a disreputable looking man, a prison guard. "That man!" exclaimed the rabbi. "Yes," said Elijah, "because he is considerate to his prisoners and refrains from cruelty. Also, since his position often brought him into contact with the authorities, he was able to keep the Jews informed of their intentions." The rabbi was thus taught that no station in life precluded a person from doing good and acting nobly.

Surveying the people rushing through the marketplace, the rabbi asked: "Who else is worthy of eternal life?" Elijah then pointed to two motley-dressed clowns who were cavorting ludicrously before an amused audience. The rabbi was astonished. "Scorn them not," admonished the prophet. "When not performing for hire, they cheer the depressed and the sorrowful. Whenever they see a sufferer, they join him and by merry talk they help him to forget his grief." Therefore, we are taught: The heart ennobles any calling. A jester may be first in the kingdom of heaven.

— adapted from Silverman,
The Sages Speak: Rabbinic Wisdom and Jewish Values,
and from Ginzberg, Legends of the Bible

Once again, common folk, whose behavior is guided by human compassion, are granted the same stature as the more traditional role models within the Jewish community. This egalitarian message is pervasive in Jewish folklore.

The Difference Between Heaven and Hell

A righteous man was permitted by God to attain foreknowledge of the world to come. In a celestial palace he was ushered into a large room, where he beheld people seated at a banquet table. The table was laden with the most delectable foods, but not a morsel had been touched. The righteous man gazed in wonder at the people seated at the table because they were emaciated with hunger, and they moaned constantly for food, even though the delicious viands were before them.

"If they are hungry, why is it that they don't partake of the food that is before them?" asked the righteous one of his heavenly guide. "They cannot feed themselves," said the guide. "If you will notice, each one has his arms strapped straight, so that no matter how he tries, he cannot get the food into this mouth." "Truly, this is hell," said the righteous one as they left the hall.

The heavenly attendant escorted him across the hall into another room, and the righteous one observed another table equally as beautiful, and laden with delicacies and delectable food. Here he noticed that those seated around the table were well fed, happy, and joyous. To his amazement he discerned that these people, too, had their arms strapped straight. Turning to his guide he asked in perplexity: "How is it then that they are so well fed, seeing that they are unable to transport the food into their mouths?"

"Behold," said the heavenly guide. The righteous one looked and he beheld that each one was feeding the other. "In truth," he exclaimed, "this is really heaven!"

"In truth it is," agreed the attendant. "As you can see, the difference between hell and heaven is a matter of cooperation and serving one's fellow."

— from Silverman,
The Sages Speak: Rabbinic Wisdom and Jewish Values

Once again, human solidarity is considered the paramount value.

In this world too, it's ethical behavior, not piety, that makes a mentsh:

A rich man, who was a profligate, a souse and a lecher, died in a certain town. The entire community mourned his death and followed his hearse to his last resting place. What a wailing, what a lamentation, was heard as his coffin was lowered into the grave! In the recollection of the oldest inhabitant no rabbi or sage had ever departed this life amidst such general sorrow.

It chanced that on the following day, another rich man died in the town. He was just the opposite of the first in character and manner of living. He was ascetic and dined on practically nothing but dry bread and turnips. He had been pious all the days of his life and sat all the time in the House of Study poring over the Talmud. Nonetheless, no one except his own family mourned his death. His funeral passed almost unnoticed, and he was laid to rest in the presence of only a handful.

A stranger, who happened to be visiting in the town at the time, was filled with wonder, and asked: "Explain to me the riddle of this town's strange behavior. It honors a profligate yet ignores a saint!"

To this one of the townsmen replied: "Know that the rich man who was buried yesterday, although he was a profligate and a drunkard, was the leading benefactor of the town. He was easy-going and merry, and loved all the good things in life. Practically everybody in this town profited from him. He'd buy wine from one, chickens from another, geese from a third, and cheese from a fourth. And, being kindhearted, he'd pay well. That's why he is missed and we mourn after him. But what earthly use was that other one, the saint, to anybody? He lived on bread and turnips and no one ever made a kopek on him. Believe me, no one will miss him!"
        — *from Ausubel, A Treasury of Jewish Folklore*

This is an adaptation from the parables of the preacher of Dubno, Rabbi Jacob Ben Wolf Kranz (1740-1804), also known as the Dubner *Maggid* (preacher). He lived in Lithuania. He was an itinerant rabbi renowned for his story-telling.

"A profligate, a souse and a lecher" may not be our ideal of a model citizen, but because of his cheerful disposition and "purchasing power," Rabbi Kranz considered him a greater asset to the Jewish community than the pious bookworm. That is quite a statement for eighteenth century Lithuania.

⌘⌘⌘

In the course of a great flood, a boatman helped a *tsaddik* (a saintly person) across a river. The holy man, seeing what an uncouth fellow the boatman was, pitied him and felt inclined to lecture him a little "My son," he said, "is this really your trade?"

"Oh, I also work on the timber rafts," said the boatman.

"But do you at least *koyveya itim letoyre?*" asked the holy man.

"What does that mean, Rebbe?"

"I'm merely asking whether you take time for studying the Torah, even so much as a chapter in the Mishnah."

"Rebbe, I can't pay expenses with the Mishnah. I have to feed my children."

"Ah, ah, ah," groaned the holy man. "A Jew without study is deprived of a quarter of his world. And I'm sorry to say that's what you've done. But tell me, do you at least recite the Psalms?"

"Rebbe, if I recited the Psalms, who'd carry the logs?"

"Ah, ah, ah," groaned the rebbe. "If only you recited the Psalms. Because a Jew who doesn't recite the Psalms has wasted another quarter of his world."

A while later the rebbe said, "Tell me, my son, do you recite your prayers?"

"A flood washed away the hut where I kept my prayer shawl and prayer book. And now I work with a troop of raftsman so I don't get to pray."

"Ah, ah, ah. So you've wasted still another quarter of your world."

Just then the boat struck a rock and capsized. "Rebbe," cried the boatman, "can you swim?"

"No," groaned the sinking rebbe.

"In that case, you've wasted all four quarters of your world. But never mind. Grab on to me and I'll pull your whole world to safety."

— *from Weinreich, Ed., Yiddish Folktales*

When a *proste Yid* (an uneducated Jew) gets the better of a *tsaddik*, we can be certain that we are hearing the voice of the common folk, not the established elites. This is the kind of subversive message that makes Jewish folklore so appealing.

Strange as it may seem, I discovered a similar folktale of Arabic origin in a biography of Karl Marx by Frances Wheen, published in 1999. Marx apparently heard the story during a trip to Algeria in 1882 and liked it so much that he included it in a letter to his daughter, Laura Lafargue. In his version, a philosopher exposes a boatman's ignorance of history and mathematics, but when the boat capsizes, the boatman makes no attempt to save the philosopher's life. If Marx knew the superior Yiddish version, he may have shown more respect for Jewish culture. He couldn't have shown less.

⌘⌘⌘

A wagon driver sought the Berdichever's [Rabbi Levi Yitzchok of Berdichev] advice as to whether he should give up his occupation because it interfered with his regular attendance at the synagogue. "Do you carry poor travelers free of charge?" asked the Rabbi. "Yes," answered the teamster. "Then you serve the Lord in your occupation just as faithfully as you would by frequenting the synagogue."

— *from Newman and Spitz, The Hasidic Anthology*

It was for good reason that Rabbi Levi Yitzchok was known as "the poor man's rabbi."

⌘⌘⌘

Among Rabbi Mendel's *hasidim* was a man by the name of
Rabbi Moshe, who was both well-to-do and fond of doing
good deeds. And then the wheel of fortune turned — to use a
popular phrase — and he lost all his money and fell into debt.
He went to the *tsaddik* and told him about his predicament.

"Go to my brother-in-law, the Seraph of Strelisk," said Rabbi
Mendel, "and pour out your heart to him."

The man did so.

When Rabbi Uri of Strelisk had heard his story he said, "I
shall take the bath of immersion [*mikva*] for you and the merit
of this bath will accrue to your benefit."

The man returned to his master and reported what had happened.

"Go back to my brother-in-law," said the rabbi of Kosov, "and
say to him: 'The bath of immersion will not serve to pay my
creditors.'"

The man rode to Strelisk a second time and said what he had
been told to.

"Very well, my son," the Seraph replied. "In that case I shall
also dedicate to your welfare the merit of the *tefilin* [phylac-
teries] which I shall put on today."

When the man repeated this in Kosov, Rabbi Mendel said:
"Give my brother-in-law this message from me: 'The *tefilin*
can't get rid of tormentors either.'"

The man did as he was bidden.

The Seraph reflected. "Well," said he, "if that is the case, I
shall do my utmost for you. I shall dedicate to you the merit of

all the prayers I say today, and thus from this hour the three merits will unite in giving you help."

Rabbi Moshe returned to Kosov and gave his report.

"Go," said the *tsaddik*, and he spoke as softly as always, only more slowly, and when he spoke slowly the effect on those who were listening was greater than if he had raised his voice. "Go speak to my brother-in-law in my name and say: 'All this will not settle a single debt.'"

When the Seraph received this message, he immediately put on his fur coat and set out for Kosov. The moment he arrived at his brother-in-law he asked: "What do you want of me?"

"What I want," said Rabbi Mendel, "is for the both of us to travel around a number of weeks and collect money from our people. For it is written: 'Thou shalt uphold him.'" And that is what they did.
— *from Buber, Tales of the Hasidim, The Later Masters, p. 96-97*

Buber (1878-1965), was a German Jewish philospher and Zionist who immigrated to Palestine in 1938, where he advocated reconciliation between the Jewish and Arab communities. He was influenced by the egalitarian message of Hasidism in formulating his "I" and "Thou" concept that posited an ongoing dialogue between man and God.

He also claimed that the Prophetic tradition was the source of values such as justice, solidarity and compassion. This story, taken from Hasidic sources, is entirely humanistic because of its emphasis on a this-worldy approach toward helping the needy.

⌘⌘⌘

One day a man who left the Jewish faith came to Rabbi Jehuda Ha-Chassid and expressed his desire to repent, but

Rabbi Jehuda sent him away.

"As little," he said, "as the staff in my hand will blossom and produce green leaves, can you hope to obtain pardon and forgiveness for your sins." But lo and behold, a few days later the staff in the Rabbi's hand began to blossom and produce green leaves! Greatly astonished at this miracle, the pious Rabbi sent for the repentant sinner and informed him of the miracle.

"Now tell me," asked Rabbi Jehuda, "have you ever rendered any service to your people?"

"Once," he said, "I came to a town inhabited by a great number of Jews. They were all in great distress, for they were being accused of a ritual murder, that is, of having murdered a Christian child for the purpose of using its blood in the Passover *matzo*. As I was no longer a Jew, I was chosen as an expert in the matter and was called upon to express my opinion before the court of justice. I could not in honor do otherwise than tell the truth. So I assured the judges that the use of human blood by Jews was absolutely impossible and diametrically opposed to all the tenets of their beliefs, and that ritual murder was an absurd myth unworthy of credence. Thanks to my arguments and evidence, the persecution of the Jews was stopped."

Thus spoke the repentant sinner, and Rabbi Jehuda no longer wondered at the miracle.

> *— adapted from Dr. Angelo S. Rappoport,*
> *The Folklore of the Jews*

Converts were recruited by Christian authorities who wished to make a case against the Jews, because they could claim intimate knowledge of Jewish law and customs. However, often their testimony was slanderous and became the basis for acts of anti-Jewish persecution. It is heartening to find a folktale where the convert does a service to the Jewish community merely by telling the truth.

Standing Up for Your Rights

In a certain Polish village there lived a Jewish tenant-farmer. He was a plain man, who had no learning, but he made up for it in piety and in good deeds. His father before him had worked the same little farm, and the landowner, a friendly old man, had lived on good terms with both father and son. Also the peasants of the countryside liked this upright tiller of the soil. They entrusted him with many of their affairs. When he went to town, which was often, they had him make purchases for them there.

One day a young nobleman arrived in the village. He had wasted his patrimony in wine, women, song and card-playing. Now he found himself without any means. Therefore, he fell upon the idea of displacing the Jew on his farm and working it himself.

"It will be an easy matter to get rid of him," he told himself. "After all, he's a Jew and am I not a nobleman?"

But things didn't go as easily as he had expected. The land-owner explained to him that he had no right to consider his proposal. Hadn't the Jew taken over the farm from his father? He paid his rent on time and in full. Why then should he take his farm away from him and leave him without bread? What the landowner didn't tell the nobleman was that he did not trust him, for he saw that he was lightheaded and irrespon-sible.

But the young nobleman didn't give up so easily. At first he tried to reach his goal in a friendly way by asking the Jew to leave the farm out of his own free will. When he saw that the Jew was stubborn and refused to oblige him, he began to

threaten him with direst misfortunes. What wouldn't he do to
him? He'd incite the peasants against him; that wouldn't be
too hard. Wasn't he a Jew? He'd inform the authorities that
certain things were not in order. He'd induce the village priest
to forbid the peasants from having any dealings with him.
And a lot of other things.

But all these threats had no effect. The Jew did not allow
himself to be intimidated. On the contrary, he went about
telling everybody in the village of the nobleman's threats.
Thereupon, both the peasants and the priest assured him that
they would ignore the rascal.

Foiled in this the nobleman conceived a devilish plan. One
day, as the Jew was on his way to town in his wagon, his
enemy, by means of money, drink and wheedling, induced
several peasant youths to wait in ambush for him in the forest
through which he had to pass.

Unaware of the danger that awaited him, the Jew got through
with all his business in town and, as dusk descended, he
started on his journey home.

The sky was overcast and it rained steadily. By the time the
Jew reached the forest, night had descended. He allowed his
horses free rein, for he could not see one step ahead of him.
Then an uneasiness fell on him. To drive away the gloom he
began to recite the psalm:

> *God is our refuge and strength, an ever-present help in
> trouble. Therefore we will not fear, though all the earth
> be removed, and though the mountains be carried into
> the midst of the sea.*

He repeated this psalm over and over again, yet the forest
continued to stretch ominous and black all around him. The

horses seemed to have lost their way and wandered aimlessly in the dark.

The Jew's uneasiness grew steadily. With increasing verve he chanted the psalm, ever louder, in order to still his fear. A thing like this had never happened to him before in his life. Times without number his horses had crossed the entire length of the forest, one could say almost blindfolded, so well they knew the way. How could he now explain the fact that they had lost their way?

At last the dawn broke. The Jew at last saw where he was and found the road back to his farm.

The young nobleman waited impatiently for the return of the peasants he had engaged to waylay the Jew. Hour after hour passed but no sign of them. When midnight came and still he had not heard from them, he grew very uneasy. The devil alone knew what had happened! Who could tell, maybe the Jew had stood up to the peasants and got the better of them! Worse yet, he could have gone and revealed everything to the authorities. Again, it was even conceivable that these rogues of peasants had betrayed him.

Stung to a frenzy by these thoughts, he got a horse and wagon and galloped off into the woods.

A thick darkness, like that which fell on Egypt under Pharaoh, lay all about him. He couldn't find his way. Suddenly, he felt a rain of blows descending on him. Several dark figures had leaped upon him, giving him no time to cry out. They belabored him so lustily that he lost his voice. When his attackers finally wearied of their exertions, he managed to find his tongue. It was then that they realized their mistake.

When the Jew finally reached home he found that all in the
village had already heard what had happened and were split-
ting their sides laughing. The young nobleman was taken to a
hospital. After that he didn't dare show his face in the village
for fear of being laughed at.

— from Ausubel, A Treasury of Jewish Folklore

Although the story implies that the Jew escaped the ambush due
to some supernatural force, a decidedly unhumanist plot twist, what
I find valuable in this story is the Jew's refusal to be intimidated.
Furthermore, he earns the respect of the Gentiles, who support
him against the nobleman. Perhaps this is because the Jew is
depicted as a farmer, living in close proximity to his Gentile neighbors. The concentration of Jews in towns, where they constituted
the merchant class, combined with their separatist religious beliefs, often placed them at odds with the Christian peasantry.

A Hasidic Folktale

A stingy tavern keeper who leased his tavern and a mill from
the local nobleman had a manservant and a maidservant who
were in love. The young couple could not marry because they
did not have enough money. The maidservant had fifty rubles
all told; and the manservant had fifty rubles all told. Each of
them was saving the money for when they would marry.

In a nearby village, there was a Jew who could not pay the
rent on his house, and the nobleman decreed that he must
hang. The man appealed to the Jewish community, crying,
"Will you see me hanged for fifty rubles?"

No one came forward to save him, however, and the day came
when the poor man was to die. Minutes before the hanging,
the two servants cried "Stop! We'll pay the fifty rubles." And
thus the man was rescued from certain death.

Someone went to the Baal Shem Tov and told him the story, but
he said, "I know about it. I'm going to see them tomorrow."

The next day the Baal Shem Tov arrived in the village and had himself driven to the tavern where the two servants worked. When he had eaten and drunk, the Baal Shem turned to the young couple and asked them why there were still unmarried. The maidservant said, "We don't have enough money." And she started to tell him the story of the fifty rubles.

The Baal Shem said, "I know all about that. But do you still want to marry this young man?"

She replied, "What's the good of saying I want to, if we haven't got the wherewithal?"

The Baal Shem Tov said, "I'll see to it that you're married." And he took them into town and saw to it that they were properly clothed and then bought them whatever else they might need for their marriage.

At the wedding, the Baal Shem asked the stingy tavern keeper what he would give the couple as a wedding present. The tavern keeper replied, "I can't give them anything. I have children of my own, and who knows what will happen to me later in life? I can't deprive my children of their inheritance."

"In that case," said the Baal Shem to the tavern keeper, "I'll give them wedding presents in your name. I'll give them the tavern and the mill."

This remark struck the man as so farfetched that he simply ignored it and walked off.

After the wedding the Baal Shem Tov invited the couple to come home with him. He told them to take a good deal of food with them. Then, just as they started out, the Baal Shem Tov suddenly disappeared, and the young couple was left alone in the countryside.

They walked and walked until they were in the middle of a
forest. There they heard someone groaning. They went closer
and the groaning got louder and louder. Suddenly, they came
upon a pit and there in the pit lay a man and a horse. When the
man saw the couple he said very weakly, "I'm hungry." So the
couple threw food down to him until he had eaten his fill and
grown strong enough to climb out of the pit.

Well, how was it that the man and the horse happened to be
there? As it turned out, he was the son of the nobleman who
owned the tavern run by the stingy tavern keeper. The
nobleman's son had been missing for three days and was
being sought everywhere. He had been on his way someplace
when he fell into the pit, and if it had not been for the young
couple, he would certainly have died of hunger.

Well, they all rode together to the nobleman's house, and
what celebration there was! The young nobleman told the
whole story of how the couple had rescued him from death. In
the evening, there was a great banquet, and the young
nobleman's mother called to the assembled company, "Let me
have your advice. What shall I give the couple who rescued
my son from death?"

All the people shouted, "Let them have the mill and the
tavern!"

And so the stingy tavern keeper and his family had to leave
their home and become beggars, while the former servants
took over the tavern and the mill and became very rich.

But that's not the end of the story. The Baal Shem Tov
wanted to test whether they still had any memory of their
earlier lives as poor folk. So he came to their village, but
before entering their house he lay down in a puddle and got
himself thoroughly dirty.

When he came into the house, a servant girl cried, "Get out of here. Just look at you, what a filthy mess you are." The former maidservant, hearing this, came running in and scolded the servant girl and asked the man to come inside and brought him food at once.

Then the disguised Baal Shem said that he wanted a place to sleep, and the former maidservant prepared a bed for him. The Baal Shem said, "I'm not going to undress. I'm going to get into bed wrapped in my coat."

"Well," said the innkeeper's wife, "never mind, just go to sleep. If the sheets get dirty, we'll wash them."

The next morning, after the Baal Shem Tov had eaten the breakfast the innkeeper's wife served him, he told the couple who he was. He blessed them with happiness and abundance, then disappeared. That's the sort of thing the Baal Shem Tov used to do.

— from Weinreich, Ed., Yiddish Folktales

This is but one of many stories about the Baal Shem Tov's good deeds and sense of justice. Most of them are also contrived to exalt his magical powers. In this story, his influence is more subtle.

The Baal Shem Tov, or its acronym, "the Besht" means Master of the Good Name. This was the title of Israel Ben Eliezer, the founder of Hasidism, who lived in the Ukraine from 1700 to1760.

He taught that ordinary Jews could achieve a direct communion with God by fervent prayer and joyful observance of the *mitsvot* (religious commandments). Because the leading rabbinic authorities elevated Talmud scholarship as the supreme value and distrusted the uneducated as potential followers of false messiahs, his ideas had enormous appeal. With so many Jews alienated from the religious establishment, the time was ripe for a popular religious revival. The Besht was its leader.

Respecting Other Opinions

There are seven characteristics of a boor and seven of a wise man. A wise man does not speak before one who has more wisdom, he does not interrupt; he thinks before he answers; his answers are relevant to the matter under discussion; he deals with first things first and last things last; he admits what he does not know; and he speaks the truth. The opposite of these are the characteristics of the boor.

— *Pirke Avot*

⌘⌘⌘

With the increase of the disciples of Shammai and Hillel who never knew the great teachers, the number of religious disputes grew and the Torah became divided.

Abba ben Shaul said: the schools of Shammai and Hillel were in conflict for three years, each side claiming to be right in its legal decisions.

Finally, a Divine echo was heard to say: both views are the expressions of the living God, nevertheless the Law is according to the School of Hillel.

The question naturally arises, if "both views are the expressions of the living God," then why was Hillel's view chosen as the decisive one? It is because the disciples of Hillel were considerate and respectful, studying not only their own opinions but also the teachings of the Shammaites. Further, they even gave precedence to the School of Shammai by quoting their views first.

Although the Schools of Shammai and Hillel were in legal conflict and what one prohibited the other frequently permitted, there was no bar on marriages between them. This is to teach you that they showed love and friendship towards one another, thus putting into practice the biblical teaching, "Love truth and peace" (*Zach. 8:19*).

— *adapted from Bialik and Ravnitzky, Stories of the Sages, from Sefer Ha'Aggadah, selected by Chaim Pearl*

Rabbis Hillel (70 B.C.E.-10 C.E.) and Shammai (first century B.C.E.) were the two great rivals of early rabbinic times. Shammai insisted on an inflexible interpretation of the law, while Hillel infused his interpretations with a keen understanding of human nature.

Followers of each school ate in each other's homes despite different interpretations of the laws of *kashrut*.

Patience

Once it came to pass that two men made a wager, the one saying that he would make Hillel angry and the other replying that it could not be done. The stake was 400 florins.

This happened on the eve of Sabbath when Hillel was washing his hair in honor of the day. The man who laid the wager that he would make Hillel angry came to the door of Hillel's house and knocked, calling out, "Where is Hillel?" Hillel covered himself with his cloak and went to meet the man and asked, "Dear son, what is your wish?" Then the man said, " I want to ask a question." Then Hillel said, "My son, ask what you desire." Whereupon the man replied, "Why are the people of Babylon round-headed?" Hillel replied, "I will tell you. There are no wise men among them, therefore they have heads in the shape of a ball." The man said, "You have given a very proper answer to my question," and went away.

A little while later he went again to Hillel's door and knocking, called out, "Where is Hillel?" The good Hillel again put on his cloak, went to meet him and said, "My son, what is your desire?" The man said, "I wish to ask you a question." Hillel said, "My son, ask what you will." Then he asked,

"Why do the people of Palmyra have round eyes?" Hillel replied, "They live in a sandy country and if they had eyes with two corners like ours, they could not remove the sand which the wind blows in their eyes and would go blind." The man said, "You have given me a very excellent answer to this question, also." And he went on his way.

After a little while he came back again, thinking he would anger Hillel by calling him so often from the bath. Again he cried, "Where is Hillel, where is Hillel?" When Hillel heard that he was being called again, he put on his cloak and went out and said, "My son, what do you wish of me?" The man said, "I want to ask you an important question." And Hillel replied, "Dear son, ask whatever question you like." Then he asked, "Tell my why the Phrygians have broad feet?" Hillel replied, "They live in swamps and they have broad soles on their feet so that they can walk about more easily, for if they had narrow feet they would sink into the swamps."

Then the man said, "I have still many more questions to ask, but I am afraid you will grow angry." Then Hillel said, "My son, ask what you like and I will answer the best I can." So he said, "Are you Hillel, whom they call the prince of Israel?" Hillel said, "Yes." Then the man said, "May there not be many like you." Hillel asked, "Why?" The man replied, "I laid a wager of 400 florins that I could make you angry and you caused me to lose." Then Hillel said, "My son, know that Hillel is well worth the 400 florins which you have lost, and you may wager another 100 florins but you still won't anger him." So the man went away.

— adapted from Moses Gaster, Ma'aseh Book

Some of Hillel's other sayings, taken from *Pirke Avot* (Ethics of the Fathers), a tractate of the Mishna, are included in this collection.

It is disconcerting to read Hillel denigrating the people of Babylon because he came from there, but his even temper and forebearance are certainly important elements of good human relations.

When a pagan asked Hillel's rival Shammai to teach him the Torah while standing on one foot, Shammai chased him away with a stick. Hillel, on the other hand, answered with his famous dictum, "What is hateful to you, do not do to others. The rest is commentary. Now go and study." Many secular humanistic Jews cite these words as their ethical foundation.

Rabbi Meir Learns from a Heretic, a.k.a., an *Apikoros*

Elisha ben Abuyah was a great rabbinic scholar of the second century C.E., who became a "heretic" (an adherent of Greek rationalism and skepticism). Seeing righteous people suffer and evil people prosper convinced him that there was no such thing as divine justice. His former colleagues referred to him as *Aher*, "the other one." Only his student, Rabbi Meir, without sharing his master's heresy, remained loyal to him until the end of his life.

For more about Elisha ben Abuyah see "But There are Alternatives to Bible and Talmud Study," in Chapter IX. An excellent historical novel about him, *As a Driven Leaf*, was written by a rabbi, Milton Steinberg.

> Rabbah bar Rabh Shilah once met the Prophet Elijah. He asked the Prophet: "With what does the Holy One, praised be He, occupy Himself?"

> Elijah answered: "He is teaching the traditions in the name of all the Rabbis, with the exception of the traditions of Rabbi Meir, in whose name He does not teach anything."

> Rabbah asked: "But why not?"

Elijah answered: "Because Rabbi Meir learned his traditions from the mouth of *Aher*."

To which Rabbah retorted: "Why should he not have done so? Rabbi Meir found a pomegranate. He ate the inside, but threw away the peel."

And the Prophet Elijah said: "Now that you have interceded on Rabbi Meir's behalf, I can actually hear the Holy One, praised be He, saying: 'My son Meir says ....'"

> — *adapted from Jakob J. Petuchowski, Ed.,*
> *Our Masters Taught: Rabbinic Stories and Sayings*

Meir was something of a liberal himself. He was a close friend of Oenomaus, a pagan philosopher, respected the beliefs of Hellenists and Samaritans and once commented that a non-Jew who studies Torah is equal to a High Priest.

In a time when talking with women was considered a waste of time at best, or a temptation to sin at worst, Meir also proved capable of respecting the opinions of his wife, Beruriah. (See "A Rabbinical Sage Learns the Law from His Wife, Chapter VII.)

Chapter IV.
The Rich and the Poor

*Nothing in the world is worse than poverty. It is the most
terrible of all burdens. ... Those crushed by poverty feel
as if all the world's troubles have been placed on their
shoulders. ... Our rabbis said: If the sufferings of the
world were gathered on one side of the scale and poverty
was on the other, poverty would outweigh them.*
  — adapted from Midrash Exodus Rabbah 31:12 and 31:14.

Why Sodom Was Destroyed

In Genesis 19, God appears to destroy Sodom because of the
sexual depravity of its inhabitants. The rabbis gave a different
explanation: it was due to equally depraved cruelty toward the
poor. They offered these tales as examples.

Our rabbis taught that the people of Sodom became cruel and
arrogant because of the wealth of their land. They said, "Since
we live in such luxury with unlimited produce, gold, silver
and precious stones in the ground, let us see to it that we get
no strangers here because they will only take away some of
our wealth." So they decided that whoever invites a stranger
to dine will lose his garments.

If a poor man passed through the city, everyone would give
him a dinar coin on which the donor scratched his own name,
but they would refuse to give or sell him any bread. When the
poor man died, each one would then come and take back his

coin. Once, a young girl gave a poor man some bread which she had hidden in a pitcher. When after three days the poor man was still alive, they found out what had happened. So they took the girl, covered her with honey and tied her fast on a rooftop, where she was stung to death by bees.

Their cruelty to the poor was equally savage. R. Judah said: an edict was passed in Sodom that whoever offers food to the poor shall be burned to death. Once two young girls went down to the well to fill their pails with water. One said to her friend, "Why do you look so pale today?" And the other answered: "We have no food and will soon die." What did the first girl do? She filled her pail with flour and they secretly exchanged pails. But as soon as the people found out that she had given away food to the poor, she was executed. Said God, "Even if I wanted to keep silent, I could not on account of the cries of this young girl."

Pelotit, Lot's daughter, was married to one of the important men of Sodom. She used to see a poor man groveling about in the street and she felt very sorry for him. So every day when she went down to the well for water she would secretly fill her pitcher with food and give it to the man. Soon enough, the people asked, "How does that poor man keep alive?" Then they found out what had happened and they brought her out for execution. The woman cried to God and asked for justice to be done to the people of Sodom.

— *adapted from Bialik and Ravnitzky, Sefer Ha-Aggadah,*
selected by Chaim Pearl

What Causes Plagues to Strike

... plagues occur in the fourth, the seventh (the Sabbatical year), the post-Sabbatical year, and at the conclusion of the feast of Sukkot. During the fourth year and seventh year, they occur for not paying the tithe to the poor; in the post-Sabbatical year, for appropriating the harvest of the Sabbatical year;

and at the conclusion of Sukkot, for robbing the poor of
various entitlements (gleanings, forgotten sheaves and the
corner crops) assigned to them in Scripture.

— Pirke Avot

According to the Torah, fields must not be cultivated every seventh year. The crops or fruit that grow of their own accord belong
to the poor. On all other years, the poor are entitled to "glean"
whatever grows on the corners of the fields and whatever is missed
during the harvesting process. The Book of Ruth, however, is the
only place in the Bible where the practice of gleaning actually
takes place.

Homeless in Imperial Rome

Rabbi Joshua ben Levi took a trip to Rome. He was astounded
to behold the magnificence of the buildings, the statues
covered with tapestry to protect them from the heat of the
summer and the cold of the winter. As he was admiring the
beauty of Roman art, a beggar plucked at his sleeve and asked
him for a crust of bread. The rabbi looked again at the statues,
and turning to the man covered with rags, he cried out: "O,
Lord, here are statues of stone covered with expensive garments. Here is a man, created in Thine own image, covered
with rags. A civilization that pays more attention to statues
than to men shall surely perish."

— from Silverman, The Sages Speak:
Rabbinic Wisdom and Jewish Values

The same observation could be made today in many of our cities,
where ragged homeless people roam the streets, while money is
poured into lavish hotels and condominiums. This is not the Jewish way. Yet how many real estate tycoons are Jewish?

Justice for the Worker and the Poor

Rabbi Wolf of Zbaraz had a stern sense of justice. Far and
wide he was famed as an incorruptible judge. One day, his

own wife raised an outcry that her maid had stolen an object of great value. The servant, an orphan, tearfully denied the accusation.

"We will let the Rabbinical Court settle this!" said her mistress angrily.

When Rabbi Wolf saw his wife preparing to go to the Court he forthwith began putting on his Sabbath robe.

"Why do you do that?" she asked in surprise. "You know it is undignified for a man of your position to come to Court with me. I can very well plead my own case."

"I'm sure you can," answered the rabbi. "But who will plead the case of your maid, the poor orphan? I must see that full justice be done to her."
                                        — from Ausubel, A Treasury of Jewish Folklore

Many philanthropists have probably failed to treat their own domestic help with respect. Although the story does show that even a servant girl has a right to a hearing in court before she could be punished, the implication is that she would not stand a chance against the rabbi's wife (rebbitsin) without an advocate of equal stature. Under these circumstances, Rabbi Wolf comes to her aid, even at the cost of marital harmony.

⌘⌘⌘

The porters engaged by Rabba Bar-Chanak broke a cask of wine belonging to him, and as a penalty he took their coats from them. They went to the sage and complained. The sage thereupon ordered Rabba to restore the garments. "Is that the law?" Rabba asked. The sage replied: "It is written, 'that thou mayest walk in the way of good men'" (Proverbs 2:20). He gave them back their coats.

The laborers then said: "We are poor and have toiled through the day and are hungry; we are in great need." The sage said to Rabba, "Go and pay their wages." Rabba asked, "Is that the law?" He replied, "Yes, for it is written, 'and keep the paths of the righteous'" (*Proverbs 2:20*).

— *from Silverman, The Sages Speak:*
Rabbinic Wisdom and Jewish Values

The unnamed sage also could have also relied on Exodus 22:24-26, which forbids taking a neighbor's only coat as collateral for a loan, and Leviticus 19:13 and Deuteronomy 24:15, which require wages to be paid daily.

The Torah envisioned a society in which the rich were forbidden to abuse the poor and the gap between them was not allowed to grow too large. Talmudic labor laws were also relatively enlightened for their time. They should not however be considered a precursor to collective bargaining, unions or laws protecting the right of workers to organize and strike. These are modern achievements for which secular-minded Jews and Christians are chiefly responsible.

⌘⌘⌘

Rabbi Israel Salanter was once invited by a former student to spend Shabbat with him. Knowing how strict his teacher was in observing the dietary laws, the student described in detail how careful he was in all matters of Jewish law. He added that in his house between each course of the Friday night meal, the participants engaged in discussions of Torah and Talmud, and sang *zmirot* (Sabbath songs).

Rabbi Salanter said that he would accept the invitation on the condition that the meal be shorter than usual. The student was surprised, but agreed, and the meal proceeded quickly. At its

end, he asked Rabbi Salanter what it was about his normal
way of conducting the meal that bothered him.

"I'll show you," replied the rabbi. He called over the maid, a
widow, and apologized to her for making her work faster than
usual.

"On the contrary," the woman smiled. "I'm grateful to you.
Friday night meals usually end very late, and I'm exhausted
from the whole week's work. Tonight, I'll be able to catch up
on some needed sleep."

After she left, Rabbi Salanter told his host that his customary
Shabbat dinner sounded fine indeed, but it shouldn't come at
the expense of his very tired maid.

— *from Telushkin, Jewish Wisdom*

Israel Salanter was an orthodox rabbi from Lithuania who lived
from 1810 to 1883. He founded the Musar, a religious movement
that taught the primacy of ethical behavior. During a plague, he
once deliberately ate in front of his congregation on Yom Kippur
to convince them not to fast. This story and the next one reflect
his reputation as a dedicated advocate for the worker and the
poor.

Rabbi Israel Salanter was very scrupulous in his observance of
all the six hundred and thirteen precepts prescribed by the
religious code. It was his custom, whenever the Passover
holidays came around, to personally supervise the baking of
matzos in his town. He wished to make sure that it was done
according to the time-honored ritual regulations.

On one such occasion, when he was confined by illness, his
disciples volunteered to supervise the baking of the matzos.

"Instruct us Rabbi," they said. "Tell us all the important things
we have to watch out for."

"My sons, see that the women who bake the matzos are well paid," was Rabbi Israel's brief reply.
— *from Ausubel, A Treasury of Jewish Folklore*

⌘⌘⌘

Rabbi Levi Yitzchok discovered that the girls who knead the dough for the unleavened bread drudged from early morning until late at night. Then he cried aloud to the congregation gathered in the House of Prayer: "Those who hate Israel accuse us of baking the unleavened bread with the blood of Christians. But no, we bake them with the blood of Jews!"
— *from Martin Buber, Tales of the Hasidim, The Early Masters*

Although Levi Yitzchok was a *Hasid* and Salanter belonged to the *Mitnagdim*, or the orthodox opponents of Hasidism, the stories about them show that they shared a common concern over the exploitation of labor. The *Hasidim*, in fact, had a high regard for Salanter.

⌘⌘⌘

A poor man once stole a piece of food and was ordered by the king to be hanged. On his way to the gallows, the man told one of the king's guards that he was in possession of a wonderful secret that he would like to reveal to the king; otherwise it would die with him. The guard took the man before the king, who asked him about the secret.

"I can put a pomegranate seed in the ground, and it will grow and bear fruit overnight," said the accused man. "It is a secret my father taught me, and I thought it would be a pity were it to die with me."

A time was appointed on the following day for planting the seed. The thief, the king, and his courtiers were all there. The thief then dug a hole and said: "This seed can be planted in the ground only by a man who never in his life has stolen or taken anything which did not belong to him. Being a thief, I cannot, of course, do it."

So the king turned to his vizier and ordered him to plant the seed. The vizier hesitated, then said, "Your Majesty, when I was a young man I recall keeping an article that did not belong to me. I, obviously, cannot plant this seed."

The treasurer, when told to plant the seed, begged the king's forgiveness, saying that dealing with such large sums of money as he did, he may have entered too much or too little in the records. The king, in his turn, recalled that he once took and kept a precious object belonging to his father.

The thief turned to them and said: "You are all mighty and powerful persons. You are not in want of anything, yet you cannot plant the seed; while I, who stole a little food to keep myself from starvation, am to be hanged."

The king, pleased with the man's clever ruse, laughed and pardoned him and sent him away with a present.
  — *from a Portion of Paradise and Other Jewish Folktales,*
translated by H.M. Nahmad

We have seen this formula before. The lowly commoner outwits the powerful ruler and saves the day. Here, however, the hero also makes the king and his advisors see that they are at least as guilty as he is. As Anatole France, the French writer said, "The law, in its majestic equality, forbids the rich as well as the poor to sleep under bridges, to beg in the streets and to steal bread."

Respect for the Dignity of the Worker and the Poor

Reb Nochemke took great pains not to hurt the sensibilities of the needy whom he aided, for he was poor himself and only too well understood the pride of the poor.

One day, he was asked to be godfather at a circumcision. Several days before the event he made inquiry and discovered that the father of the infant was in bad financial circumstances and had no money for the celebration. So Reb Nochemke went to see him.

"When, my son, are you planning to go to Kovno?" Reb Nochemke asked him.

"Why Kovno, Reb Nochemke? Who's going to Kovno?" asked the man, astonished.

"I thought that maybe you were going to Kovno," answered Reb Nochemke, lamely.

"And what if I was going to Kovno?" inquired the man, curiously.

"Well, if you were going I wanted to ask a favor of you. I owe a man who lives there twenty-five rubles and so I wanted you to pay him for me."

"But Reb Nochemke, how do I know when I'll be going to Kovno? I haven't been there for two years."

"There's no particular hurry! The man can wait. Just the same, here are the twenty-five rubles and the next time you do go to Kovno I'll be much obliged to you if you give it to him. On the other hand, should the money come in handy to you in the meantime you're welcome to use it. You can replace it later."

Unsuspecting, the man took the twenty-five rubles and was glad. He spent the money on the circumcision party and he was not obliged to feel humiliated, as he had feared all along.

When Reb Nochemke arrived at the circumcision the father said to him anxiously, "You forgot to give me the name and address of the man in Kovno for whom you gave me the money."

"Let me see, now," answered Reb Nochemke, as if trying to recall. "No, I'm afraid I can't remember. I have the name and address at home and I'll let you know some other time."

But this other time never came around, for Reb Nochemke said he had mislaid the address. After a while, the poor man scraped together the twenty-five rubles and returned them to Reb Nochemke.

— from Ausubel, A Treasury of Jewish Folklore

Reb Nachum (Nochemke) Grudner was a preacher who lived in Grodno, Lithuania (1811-1879) whose devotion to the poor became the subject of legends. Here Reb Grudner disguises an act of charity so well that the recipient takes it as a loan.

⌘ ⌘ ⌘

The rabbi watched his servant girl panting under the burden of the yoke from which hung two buckets of water. At mealtime, before he sat down to eat with his disciples, he washed his hands using very little water.

"Why are you so economical with the water, Rabbi?" asked one of his disciples.

The rabbi smiled and said, "While it is an act of piety to wash one's hands before meals, I must not be pious at my servant girl's expense."

— from Ausubel, A Treasury of Jewish Folklore

Undoubtedly, this is yet another story about Rabbi Israel Salanter who taught that ethical behavior took priority over ritual observance.

⌘⌘⌘

The son of Rabbi ben Matthias hired several laborers and
promised them their meals. His father said: "It would have
been better had you given them their full compensation in
money and let them buy their own meals ... for a worker is
entitled to eat what he himself prefers."
                      — *from Browne, Ed., The Wisdom of Israel*

Well-compensated workers are still the equivalent of servants if
they do not enjoy a modicum of autonomy on the job. One of the
most powerful reasons why workers join unions is to secure digni-
fied treatment from their employers. With our roots in the Jewish
labor movement, this is a lesson that Secular Humanistic Jews
must not forget.

Maimonides' Eight Degrees of Charity

There are eight degrees or steps, says Maimonides, in the duty
of charity. The first and lowest degree is to give, but with
reluctance or regret. This is the gift of the *hand*, but not of the
heart.

The second is to give cheerfully, but not proportionately to the
distress of the sufferer.

The third is to give cheerfully and proportionately, but not
until we are solicited.

The fourth is to give cheerfully, proportionately, and even
unsolicited; but to put it in the poor man's hand, thereby
exciting in him the painful emotion of shame.

The fifth is to give charity in such a way that the distressed
may receive the bounty and know their benefactor, without
their being known to him. Such was the conduct of some of

our ancestors, who used to tie up money in the hind-corners of
their cloaks, so that the poor might take it unperceived.

The sixth, which rises still higher, is to know the objects of
our bounty, but remain unknown to them. Such was the
conduct of those of our ancestors who used to convey their
charitable gifts into poor people's dwellings, taking care that
their own persons and names should remain unknown.

The seventh and still more meritorious, namely, to bestow
charity in such a way that the benefactor may not know the
relieved persons, nor they the name of their benefactor. This
was done by our charitable forefathers during the existence of
the Temple. For there was in that holy building a place called
the Chamber of Silence or Inostentation; wherein the good
deposited secretly whatever their generous hearts suggested;
and from which the most respectable poor families were
maintained with equal secrecy.

Lastly, the eighth and most meritorious of all, is to anticipate
charity by preventing poverty; namely, to assist the reduced
brother, either by a considerable gift, or a loan of money, or
by teaching him a trade, or by putting him in the way of
business, so that he may earn an honest livelihood and not be
forced to the dreadful alternative of holding up his hand for
charity. And to this Scripture alludes when it says, "And if thy
brother be waxen poor and fallen in decay with thee, then
though shalt support him: Yea though he be a stranger or a
sojourner, that he may live with thee" (*Leviticus 25:35*). This
is the highest step and the summit of charity's Golden Ladder.
— *from Ausubel, A Treasury of Jewish Folklore*

Maimonides (1135-1204), a.k.a., Moses ben Maimon or the
Rambam, is widely recognized as one of the greatest Jewish phi-
losophers and legal codifiers. He lived in Spain and Egypt. His
crowning achievement, *Guide for the Perplexed*, was an attempt

to reconcile Judaism with Aristotelian rationalism. His *Thirteen Articles of Faith*, however, are anything but rational. Including precepts such as "God is eternal," "Only He may be worshiped," "The Torah is immutable," and "God will reward the just and punish the wicked," they remain at the core of rabbinic Judaism.

Helping Those in Need

Once there lived a man whose name was Job. He built himself a house that had four entrances, one on each side. He did this, thinking "When the poor and the hungry come let them quickly find my door."

Whenever a hungry man came Job hastened to bring him food and drink. For these deeds of loving kindness to his fellow-men, God blessed Job: He made him rich and his fame spread throughout the land. Despite his good fortune, Job remained modest and pious as before.

It chanced that a poor man died and left behind him a helpless widow and many orphans. When Job heard of this he said to himself: "I will go to the poor woman to console and help her." At that very instant an angel of Evil rose up before him. But he came in the disguise of one of Job's friends so that the good man did not recognize him for what he really was.

"I've heard," said the angel, "that you wish to comfort the poor widow whose husband has just died. I've hastened here to keep you from going to her."

"Why do you come to mock at me?" asked Job.

"How can you stoop so low as to visit the widow of a poor man!" cried the angel of Evil. "You are the foremost man among your people and its judge, and you must jealously guard the great dignity of your position."

"Hold your peace!" spoke Job sternly. "I will call on this widow none the less. Do you think I am better than God who comforts the widows and the orphans?"

When the angel heard this he departed.

Job went to see the woman; he spoke words of consolation to her and her children. Afterwards he inquired from her neighbors whether her late husband had left her anything, field or vineyard.

"No," they told him, "this man owned only a small field that, in recent, years gave no yield."

Job decided, therefore, to help the woman.

When the seven days of mourning were ended he went to call on the widow and told her, "When you get ready to cultivate your field, I will send you one of my servants and two donkeys to help you."

"Far be it from me to accept aid from a strange man!" she answered him. "God, the father of all orphans, will have mercy on me and my children. He will not abandon us in our need."

"At least let me plant for you a vegetable garden," asked Job.

But this help too she rejected.

When sowing-time arrived the woman sold all her household goods. With the money she rented a donkey and cultivated her field. But the results were disappointing; the ground gave forth only thorns and thistles. The poor woman and her children were obliged to go hungry that winter.

When Job heard of her misfortune he sent her grain to last her for a whole year. But she refused to accept it.

"I will hire myself out as a servant," she sent word to Job, "so that I and my children may live by the labor of my own hands."

The widow went to work for another but her wages were far from enough to feed her and her children. So they continued to feel the pangs of hunger.

When Job heard of this his heart grew heavy, and he made a resolve. He let it be known far and wide that the widow was his own blood-relation.

When the people heard of this, they said, "Happy the man who will be lucky enough to marry this woman; he will inherit some of Job's wealth."

And so it happened. A righteous man married the widow, and Job helped him with a lavish hand. The newly wedded couple lived in happiness and peace.

Now it happened that many other men died during that time and a great number of children became orphans. These, too, Job wished to help but when he tried to give them food and clothing and offered to sow their fields, they refused his aid. So Job said to his servants, "Take your tools and cultivate the fields of these unfortunates who don't want to accept my help. Should they try to prevent you, pay no attention to them but go on with your work."

When the servants of Job tried to cultivate their fields the widows and the orphans arose to drive them away.

"Who asked you to cultivate our field?" they protested.

But Job's servants followed their master's instructions and paid no attention to them. In fact, they were obliged to resist them with force.

The inhabitants of the countryside soon heard the news. Then they spoke with bitterness, "What conduct for a pious man like Job! He has seized by violence the fields of helpless orphans! He ignores the rights of the people and does as he pleases! Indeed, he is not pious and good as we always thought, but a wretched hypocrite!"

In this manner Job was slandered, and no one esteemed him anymore as they had done before.

But when harvest-time came around, the servants of Job gathered in all the crops and gave them to the orphans. Those who had reviled him before saw how unjust they had been to him, and they were very contrite.
                            — *from Ausubel, A Treasury of Jewish Folklore*

The biblical Job was also a righteous man, but God and Satan contrived to make his life miserable. This Job has a different problem. He must learn how to help poor people too proud to accept charity. Rather than give up after being rebuffed, he devises subtle, but more effective methods to realize his worthy intentions.

⌘⌘⌘

A rich *Hasid* once came to Dov Baer, the Maggid of Mezritch, and asked for his blessing.

"How do you eat each day?" asked the Maggid.

"With great simplicity," answered the rich man. "I eat only dry bread with a little salt."

"Dry bread and salt!" exclaimed the Maggid. "Why don't you treat yourself to meat and wine since you are so wealthy?"

The Maggid continued to chastise the man until he promised to start eating a more expensive diet.

After he had left, the Maggid's disciples asked him, "What difference does it make whether he eats dry bread or meat?"

"It matters a great deal," answered the Maggid. "If he is used to rich foods, then he will understand that a poor man must at least have a dry crust with a little salt. But if he is only used to dry bread and salt, he will imagine that the poor can content themselves with stones."
— *from Frankel, The Classic Tales, 4000 Years of Jewish Lore*

There is a huge difference between choosing to live an ascetic live and being forced to live without material comforts. The *rebbe* in this story, Dov Baer of Mezritch (1710-1772), became the leader of the Hasidic movement upon the death of the Baal Shem Tov. He knew that people who are absorbed in acts of self-denial are unlikely to think about the welfare of others.

What's Worse than Not Helping

Two charitable men went from house to house collecting alms for their poor neighbor. Finally, they came upon two wealthy men drinking tea. One of them was forthright and bluntly said that he would make no donation. "I don't believe in charity," he declared. The other began to inquire in great detail about the poor man, as to how old he was, whether he had a wife and children, what kind of house they lived in, and similar matters.

The charity collectors were delighted with him, seeing how intensely interested he was in the affairs of the poor man.

"Who can tell," they thought hopefully, "this good man might give us a ruble, maybe even five!"

But the poor man proposes and the rich man disposes. After the rich man was through with his thorough questioning, he remarked with disgust, "That man you're gathering alms for is a swindler! He is lazy and a drunkard. I don't give away money to lazy drunkards."

Thereupon the charity collectors arose and said with scorn, "Your friend told us plainly he did not wish to give a donation because he did not believe in charity. Well and good, he has a right to do as he pleases. But how dare you, who never had the intention of giving in the first place, insult and slander an unfortunate poor man!"

MORAL: A wicked man, who does not wish to help the unfortunate will speak evil of them to cover up his guilty conscience.

— from Ausubel, A Treasury of Jewish Folklore

As they say in Yiddish, *gut gezugt* (well said).

How to Deal with Skinflints ...

In the time of famine a *tsaddik* [*i.e.*, a righteous saintly person] took it upon himself to raise money enough to feed all the starving people in the community. In the course of his rounds he approached a certain rich man who was notoriously boorish and ill tempered. Instead of receiving alms, however, all the *tsaddik* got from him was a slap in his face. The holy man was dazed for a moment; but then, wiping the blood from his cheek, he said gently; That, my son, was evidently meant for me. Now what will you give for my poor?"

— from Browne, Ed., The Wisdom of Israel

"Turning the other cheek" is said to be a Christian concept, but, in this story, the *tsaddik*, like Jesus, returns violence with equanimity in order to serve a higher purpose.

⌘⌘⌘

A rich miser, having lost his purse, announced that he would give a generous reward to the finder. When a poor man showed up with it, the miser counted the contents and immediately cried: "There are a hundred rubles missing! Go away, man! Would you expect me to give you a reward yet?"

The other, knowing he had taken nothing out of the purse, complained to the local *tsaddik*, who sent for the skinflint and demanded: "How much did your purse contain?" "Five hundred rubles," came the brazen reply.

Turning to the poor man, the *tsaddik* asked. "And how much was in the purse that you found?"

"Four hundred rubles," he answered meekly.

"Then it is clear," the *tsaddik* decided, turning back to the miser, "that this purse was not the one you lost. You will therefore give it back to the finder and let him keep it until its rightful owner appears!"
                              — *from Browne, Ed., The Wisdom of Israel*

This is the kind of behavior that one would expect from a *tsaddik*, but what is remarkable about this story is that he carries enough authority in the community to overrule the rich miser.

... and with a "Welfare Cheat"

One day Rabbi Johanan and Rabbi Simeon ben Lakish went to bathe in the public baths of Tiberias. They met a poor man who asked for charity. They said, "When we come back."

When they returned, they found him dead. They said, "Since we showed him no charity when he was alive, let us attend to him now that he is dead." When they were laying him out for burial, they found a purse full of silver pieces upon him. Then they remembered what Rabbi Abbahu had said, "We must show charity even to the deceivers, for were it not for them, a man might be asked for alms by [one who is really] a poor man, and he might refuse" (*T.J. Pe'ah, 8:9 [Jerusalem Talmud]*).
— *from Montefiore and Loewe, A Rabbinic Anthology*

Those who take charity or government assistance without really needing it may offend our sense of fairness, but for every person who cheats, are there not hundreds in dire need who cannot obtain help? The word *tsedaka* means more than charity. It means "justice."

The Light Side: The Miracle of the Broken Leg

No one showed any compassion for the poor man as he went from house to house begging for a groschen or a crust of bread. Many a door was slammed in his face and he was turned away with insults. Therefore he grew despondent.

One wintry day, as he was trudging through the slippery streets, he fell and broke his leg. Thereupon they took him to a hospital.

When the people of the town heard that a poor stranger had been taken to the hospital suffering from a broken leg, they began to feel very sorry for him. Some went to comfort him, others brought him good things to eat. When he left the hospital they furnished him with warm clothes and gave him a tidy sum of money.

Before the poor man left town he wrote to his wife, "Praise God, dear wife! A miracle happened: I broke a leg!"
— *from Ausubel, A Treasury of Jewish Folklore*

Chapter V.
The Dangers of
Fanaticism

If you are holding a sapling in your hand and someone
tells you the Messiah has come, plant the sapling first,
then go look for the Messiah.
> — *Rabbi Yohanan ben Zakkai*
> *from The Fathers According to Rabbi Nathan,*
> *a minor tractate of the Talmud, similar to Pirke Avot,*
> *compiled by a second century C.E. rabbi, judge and scholar*

The Destruction of the Second Temple

In Jewish religious tradition, the tragedies that have befallen the Jewish people are usually attributed to God's punishment for their failure to obey the Law. In this way, the rabbis could preserve the illusion that the Jews remained the Chosen People who would receive their reward with the coming of the Messiah, if only they were worthy. This approach presents profound moral problems for many reasons. It depicts God as vengeful, exonerates the real guilty parties from their crimes against the Jewish people and promotes Jewish passivity in the face of enemy attacks. However, in the case of the first Jewish revolt against Rome (68-72 C.E.), which caused massive destruction and culminated in the destruction of the Second Temple, the rabbis took a more sophisticated approach.

The reference to "groundless hatred" in the first selection is explained in the second, where it becomes clear that fanaticism among the Jewish rebels vastly contributed to the catastrophe. Indeed, it was the compromisers, represented by Yohanan ben Zakkai, rather than the militants, represented by the Zealots, that guaranteed the survival of the Jewish people. The third selection, which appears to simplistically blame the Jews for their own misfortunes, is actually an allegory on the sectarianism and internal strife that plagued Judea at the time of the Roman onslaught. Indeed, as the three selections reveal, "groundless hatred" and "overzealousness" triumphed over simple human decency and good common sense.

> Why was the first Temple destroyed [in 586 B.C.E.]? Because of three offenses committed [by the Jews of that period]: idolatry, sexual immorality, and murder. ... But why then was the second Temple destroyed [in 70 C.E.], given that the Jews of that time studied Torah, kept the commandments and performed acts of charity? Because groundless hatred was prevalent. This teaches us that the offense of groundless hatred is equivalent of the three sins of idolatry, sexual immorality and murder (*Babylonian Talmud, Yoma 9b*).
>
> — *from Telushkin, Jewish Wisdom*

⌘ ⌘ ⌘

Vespasian [the Roman general] attacked Jerusalem and he set siege to it for three years. There were three very rich men living in Jerusalem at the time. One of them offered to supply the Jerusalemites with wheat and barley. Another offered wine, salt and oil, while the third volunteered to supply the people with wood. These men opened their storehouses and it was reckoned that they had sufficient stock to keep the people in supplies for twenty-one years.

The Zealots were then around and the sages said, "Let us make peace with the Romans." But the Zealots would not let them and argued the opposite, "Let us fight them." The rabbis advised against it saying that nothing would be gained.

Whereupon the Zealots burned down the storehouses and the city was gripped by famine.

Rabbi Johanan ben Zakkai went out into the streets, and he saw some Jerusalemites boiling straw and drinking the water. When he saw this he exclaimed, "It's impossible for these people to stand up to Vespasian's army." Immediately, he decided to get out of the city and see what he could do.

Abba Sikra ben Batiah, the leader of the Jerusalem Zealots, was a nephew of R. Johanan b. Zakkai. The latter sent word to him to come secretly to see him. When he arrived, R. Johanan said, "How long will you people continue with this mad policy and starve us all out?" Abba Sikra replied "What can I possibly do? If I so much as suggest an alternative, they would kill me." At this, R. Johanan said, "Devise some way to get me out of here; perhaps I can save something from the situation." Abba Sikra replied that the city defenders had resolved not to let anyone out of the city alive. "Then pretend that I am dead" said R. Johanan. "In that case," answered the rebel leader, "spread the word that you are critically ill and everyone will come to visit. Bring into your room something that smells foul so that people will get the impression that you are dead and your body is already putrefying. Then tell your disciples to come in and carry you away in your coffin, but be careful to let no one else come near in case they should guess from the lighter weight of a living body that the whole thing is a hoax."

R. Johanan followed the plan and summoned his trusted disciples Rabbi Eliezer and Rabbi Joshua and said "My children, make a coffin for me to lie in and carry me out of here." When all was ready, R. Eliezer took the head and R. Joshua took the feet and so they carried their master until they reached the city gates at sunset. When they came to the guard point, the men at the gate demanded "Who is there?" The rabbis answered "We carry out the dead since it is not permitted to bury him within the city." The Zealots were about to thrust a sword through the coffin to test the story, but Abba Sikra called out "No, people will be appalled that we thrust the sword through their teacher!" Then some of them wanted just to shove the body around but again Abba Sikra prevented this as disrespectful to their master. Finally they opened the gate and allowed the mournful procession through.

— adapted from Bialik and Ravnitsky, Sefer Ha-Aggadah,
selected by Chaim Pearl

Rabbi Johanan ben Zakkai (first century C.E.) received permission from Vespasian to establish a rabbinical academy in the town of Yavne, which became the new center of Jewish life after the fall of Jerusalem.

⌘⌘⌘

The destruction of Jerusalem brought about by Kamza and Bar Kamza occurred as follows. A certain man had a friend named Kamza and an enemy named Bar Kamza. Once when he was making a party he said to his servant, "Go and bring Kamza." The servant went and brought Bar Kamza. The host found Bar Kamza seated among the invited guests and said to him, "You are my enemy! What are you doing here? Get up and leave!" The humiliated man pleaded, "Since I am already here, let me stay and I will pay for whatever I eat and drink at your party." "No!" was the answer. "I will pay for half the cost of the party." The reply again was "No." "I will pay all the costs of the party," said Bar Kamza. "No," replied the host, and taking Bar Kamza by the hand he pulled him up and put him out.

Bar Kamza thought to himself: "The rabbis were sitting there and did not intervene; evidently the incident did not bother them. Therefore I shall go and inform against them to the Roman emperor." He went and told the emperor, "The Jews are rebelling against you." The ruler said, "Prove it!" He answered, "Send them a sacrifice and see if they will accept it." He sent a calf of fine quality. While it was on the way, Bar Kamza made a blemish on it [to make it unacceptable according to Jewish law].

The rabbis were inclined to accept it so as not to offend the government, but Rabbi Zechariah ben Avkulus said to them, "People will say that animals with blemishes may be sacrificed on the altar." Then they thought they should kill Bar Kamza so that he should not again inform the authorities. But R. Zechariah ben Avkulus said to them, "Is one who blemishes an animal to be executed for it?"

It was about this that Rabbi Johanan remarked, "The overzealousness of R. Zechariah ben Avkulus led to the destruction of the Temple. Rabbi Eleazar said, "See how serious a thing it is to embarrass a person. For the Holy One took up the cause of Bar Kamza and burned down His Temple."

> — adapted from Judah Nadich,
> The Legends of the Rabbis, Vol. I,
> Jewish Legends of the Second Commonwealth

Life Must Go On

When the Second Temple was destroyed, many in Israel became ascetics, committing themselves not to eat meat or drink wine. Rabbi Joshua approached them and said, "My children, why do you not eat meat or drink wine?"

They answered, "Shall we eat meat, which used to be offered on the altar as a sacrifice, now that the altar has ceased to exist? Shall we drink wine, which used to be poured as a libation on the altar, now that it is poured no longer?"

He said to them, "In that case, we should stop eating bread, since the meal offerings have ceased."

"We will get by on fruit," they answered.

"But we cannot eat fruit," Rabbi Joshua said, "because the offering of the first fruits has ceased." [This is a reference to the way Shevuos was celebrated when the Temple still stood.]

"We will eat the other kinds of fruit, which do not require an offering at the Temple."

"But in that case we ought not to drink water because the pouring of the water on the altar [during Succos] has ceased."

They were silent.

He then said to them, "My children, come and let me advise you. Not to mourn at all is impossible, because of the destruction that has befallen us. But to mourn too much is also impossible because we are forbidden to impose a decree on the community that the majority will find unbearable" (*Babylonian Talmud, Bava Bathra 60b*).
                                                    — *from Telushkin, Jewish Wisdom*

This principle — not to impose a decree on the community that the majority will find unbearable — is a powerful deterrent to fanaticism, and one that some of today's rabbis, here and in Israel, appear to have forgotten.

⌘⌘⌘

Rabbi Simeon bar Yochai [who was under a death sentence for opposing Roman rule], together with his son, took refuge in the schoolhouse. Every day Simeon's wife would bring them a loaf of bread and a pitcher of water. After a few weeks, the Roman oppression became worse and Simeon said to his son, "We cannot rely on womenfolk for our safety. If the Romans should torture your mother she could reveal our whereabouts and then we are all lost."

They found a cave and they hid there. By a miracle, a well of water sprang up and a locust tree gave them fruit to sustain them. In order to preserve their clothes they would strip and bury themselves in the sand up to their necks; except for the time of prayer when they would put on their clothes. All day long they occupied themselves with the study of Torah.

They remained in that cave for twelve years. Then one day the prophet Elijah stood outside the cave and called, "Tell Rabbi Simeon that the Roman emperor is dead and that all his former decrees have been annulled." Hearing this, the two of them came out from the cave and began to walk around. Seeing people ploughing and sowing their fields they remarked, "These people are forsaking life eternal and grasping instead the things that are material and only temporary." Their furious indignation at some of the things they saw resulted in the destruction of whatever their critical eye fell upon. In due course, a heavenly voice declared, "If you have come to destroy the world, then it were better for you to go back to your cave!"
    — *adapted from Bialik and Ravnitsky, Stories of the Sages,*
            from Sefer Ha'Aggadah, selected by Chaim Pearl

Rabbi Simeon bar Yochai (mid-second century C.E.) was a fanatic in other ways. He became so embittered against non-Jews that he declared: "Kill the best of Gentiles." His son, Eleazar ben Simeon, reacted against his father's views by working for the Romans. (See the first story under "Non-Cooperation" in Chapter II.)

According to some versions of Pirke Avot, Simeon also said that anyone who interrupts Torah study to admire the beauty of nature deserves to die. The Hebrew poet and Zionist, Micha Joseph Berdichevsky, writing at the turn of the twentieth century, insisted that this contempt for the natural world among traditional religious Jews threatened the survival of the Jewish people.

Wrong Priorities

The Yehudi once told his disciple Rabbi Bunam to go on a journey. Bunam did not ask any questions but left town with a number of *Hasidim* and just followed the highway. Toward noon they came to a village and stopped at an inn. The inn-keeper was so pleased with his pious guests that he invited them to have dinner with him. Rabbi Bunam sat down in the main room, while the others went in and out and asked all sorts of questions concerning the meat which was to be served them: whether the animal was unblemished, what the butcher was like, and just how carefully the meat had been salted. At that a man dressed in rags spoke up. He had been sitting behind the stove and still had his staff in his hand. "Oh you *Hasidim*," he said, "you make a big to-do about what you put into your mouths being clean, but you don't worry half as much about the purity of what comes out of your mouths!"

Rabbi Bunam was about to reply, but the wayfarer had already disappeared – for this is Elijah's habit. Then the rabbi under-stood why his teacher had sent him on this journey.
— *From Buber, Tales of the Hasidim, The Later Masters, p. 229*

Elijah appears in many Jewish folktales as someone who pro-vides help to the unfortunate or teaches a moral lesson. Interest-ingly, Elijah's role in the Bible (see 1 Kings 17 - 2 Kings 2) bears little resemblance to the role he plays in Jewish folklore. Perhaps he became a central figure in folklore because he is one of only two figures in the Bible who does not die. As told in 2 Kings 2, God takes him up to heaven in a "whirlwind." According to Talmu-dic tradition, he will return to earth to usher in the Messiah.

Chapter VI.
Jewish Humor

Humor in Jewish tradition is typically viewed as a survival tool invented by a people accustomed to living in hostile environments. Since Jews lacked the power to overcome the indignities they suffered, they released their frustrations by mocking their own foibles.

There is a good deal of truth to this perspective, but it is incomplete. It fails to take into account the divisions within the Jewish community between the rabbis and the wealthy on the one hand and the *proste mentshen* (the common people) and the *apikorsim* (heretics or skeptics) on the other. The prevailing religious ideology taught that Jews ought to accept their fate and pray for the coming of the Messiah, but many Jews, usually the poorer ones, could not suppress their discontent with the status quo. This discontent was often manifested in the irreverent, ironic outlook on life that became the hallmark of Jewish humor.

As Sholem Aleichem, the greatest Jewish humorist, said, "To ridicule is a Jewish quality. ... When is a Jew not inclined to joke, not God forbid, out of joy, but on the contrary, because of troubles, poverty, sickness and worries about making a living? There is not greater pleasure than to stand in the street or in the synagogue and laugh at the leaders of the community, the rich men. ... Jewish legend has created many wits and jokers. The stories about them, and in their name, are often profound and cutting and dipped in the acid known as satire."

Indeed, this is humor with a humanist *taam* (flavor).

Poking Fun at the Pious

In a certain town a woman died. So they buried her. But the following morning, what was the amazement of the town folk when they discovered that the woman had been cast out of her grave! "The earth has rejected her!" lamented the pious women of the town.

So they went to the rabbi to hear his opinion.

The rabbi searched among all his holy books and found the explanation. "The wretched woman neglected to bake her *khale* according to our ancient rites," he said.

"What shall we do with her?" asked the women.

"Pile up wood and burn her!" ordered the rabbi.

But when they threw the body into the flames the fire would not consume it. "What is wrong now?" wailed the women.

"The wretch!" stormed the rabbi. "She neglected to light the Sabbath candles as our Holy Law bids! Therefore the fire won't have her either."

"What shall we do now?" asked the women.

"Cast the body into the river!" ordered the rabbi.

So the women took large stones and tied them to the corpse and threw it into the river! But the water rejected it and cast it out upon the shore.

"The wretch!" raged the rabbi. "She neglected to bathe regularly in the *mikva* according to our ancient rites. Therefore the water doesn't want her, either."

When the women heard what the rabbi said they broke into loud lamentation.

"Hush! You silly women!" the rabbi admonished them. "What are you wailing about? Surely you're all pious women! You've observed all the commandments and regulations when you baked the *khale*, lit the Sabbath candles and bathed in the *mikva*. Take my word for it, you'll not suffer the fate of this miserable woman! The earth will hold you, the fire will consume you, and the water will accept you!"
— *from Ausubel, A Treasury of Jewish Folklore*

⌘⌘⌘

An atheist once came to see a wonder-working rabbi [*i.e.* a Hasidic rebbe].

"Sholem aleichem, Rabbi," said the atheist.

"Aleichem sholem," answered the rabbi.

The atheist took a gulden and handed it to him. The rabbi pocketed it without a word.

"No doubt you've come to see me about something," he said, "Maybe your wife is childless and you want me to pray for her?"

"No, Rabbi, I'm not married," replied the atheist.

Thereupon, he gave the rabbi another gulden. Again the rabbi pocketed the gulden without a word.

"But there must be something you wish to ask me," he said. "Possibly you've committed a sin and you'd like me to intercede with God for you."

"No, Rabbi, I don't know of any sin I've committed," replied the atheist.

And again he gave the rabbi a gulden and again the rabbi pocketed it without a word.

"Maybe business is bad and you want me to bless you?" asked the rabbi, hopefully.

"No, Rabbi, this has been a prosperous year for me," replied the atheist.

Once more the atheist gave him a gulden.

"What do you want of me, anyway?" asked the rabbi, a little perplexed.

"Nothing, just nothing," replied the atheist. "I merely wished to see how long a man can go on taking money for nothing!"
— *from Ausubel, A Treasury of Jewish Folklore*

⌘⌘⌘

Two disciples were bragging about the relative merits of their wonder-working rabbis. One said, "Once my rabbi was traveling on the road when suddenly the sky became overcast. It began to thunder and to lightning and a heavy rain fell, a real deluge. What does my rabbi do? He lifts up his eyes to Heaven, spreads his hands in prayer and immediately a miracle happens! To the right darkness and a downpour, to the left, darkness and a downpour. But in the middle, clear sky and the sun is shining!"

"Call that a miracle?" sneered the other disciple. "Let me tell you what happened to my rabbi. "Once he was riding in a wagon to a nearby village. It was on a Friday. He remained

longer there than he intended and, on his way back, he found
that night was falling. What was to be done? He couldn't very
well spend the Sabbath in the middle of the field, could he?
So he lifted his eyes to Heaven, spread out his hands to right
and left, and immediately a miracle took place! To the right of
him stretched the Sabbath, to the left of him stretched the
Sabbath – but in the middle it was Friday!"

— from Ausubel, A Treasury of Jewish Folklore

⌘⌘⌘

Once Teltza, the beautiful only daughter of Shmuel the
Shingle-Maker and Dvarshe the Midwife, was sweeping the
floor of their poor house when she began to imagine her
future.

"Here I am," she thought, "fifteen years old and beloved of
everybody. I'm young and pretty and happy as a lark. In a
year or two Papa will find me a fine young scholar, and we'll
be married with song, dance and a delicious feast to which the
whole town will be invited. A year later I'll give birth to a
fine, healthy son, and what a grand party we'll have at his
bris! And then will come his *bar mitsva*. But, oh, no! What if
he cries: 'My head, my head!' and dies like the son of the
Shunnamite in the Bible?"

Teltza dropped her broom and began to weep bitterly. "If he
dies, I will surely die of sorrow! Imagine, dead at thirteen!"

Her mother heard her crying and came running. "My daughter, what is the matter?"

"Oh, Mama!" cried Teltza. "I was imagining my son's *bar
mitsva* and then I thought: 'What if he dies? I will surely die
of sorrow!'"

When she heard this, her mother raised her hands to heaven and began to wail even louder than her daughter.

Her father heard them crying and came running. When they told him why they were crying, he too joined in, and the three of them made so much noise that even the grandmother, who was hard of hearing, came to investigate. Soon she, too, was weeping and wringing her hands.

In a short time word spread throughout Chelm that a great disaster had befallen Teltza and her family. Soon all the people of the town came running to express their sympathy, and they began crying together with the grieving family. Along came the rabbi and asked them why they were all crying.

"Some great calamity has struck the family," they told him.

"There is only one thing to do," declared the rabbi. "We must all chant Psalms to avert the disaster."

So they all began to chant Psalms, beseeching the heavens to have mercy on these poor people.

Then along came the miller, the only person in town who had not been born in Chelm. He asked them why they were crying.

"Some terrible disaster has struck these poor people!" they replied.

"What has happened?" the miller asked.

But nobody could say exactly what had happened. So the miller sought out Teltza and asked her.

With a voice choked with sobs, she told him her sad tale.

The miller threw back his head and laughed. "What a silly girl you are! Your sorrow is based on four great 'ifs'— if you marry, and if you have a son, and if he gets sick on his *bar mitsva*, and if he dies. But none of these things has happened!"

Instantly Teltza stopped crying and smiled. When the others saw this, they too stopped their tears and broke into smiles. Soon everyone was laughing and slapping each other on the back.

"You see, my fellow Jews," beamed the rabbi, "nothing helps in a time of trouble like chanting Psalms. It never fails!"
— *from Frankel, The Classic Tales, 4000 Years of Jewish Lore*

Chelm, as you probably know, was the legendary town of fools. The story of the son of the Shunnamite women is found in II Kings 4:8-27. A boy dies after experiencing severe head pain and is miraculously revived by the prophet Elisha.

The Witty vs. the Wealthy

Once, on a Thursday, Hershel Ostropolier came to his rabbi to ask from him money for the Sabbath. It had been definitely agreed that the rabbi was to pay him weekly wages. Had he not imported Hershel from Ostropolier to Miedziboz to serve as his jester in order to help him drive away his depression? But the rabbi, who was ill-natured and tight-fisted, was reluctant to pay him his wages. Hershel had to resort to all kinds of stratagems to collect from him. Many a time, he and his wife and his children were forced to go hungry and did not have the wherewithal to observe the Sabbath with decency.

"What do you think, money grows on trees?" the rabbi said at first. Afterwards, when he saw that Hershel was determined, he put on a cheerful face and said to him, "If you'll tell me a good story I'll try and find you a couple of gulden to buy food for the Sabbath."

Hershel almost burned up on hearing these words. He lusted for revenge! He thought the matter over and finally told the rabbi the following story: "Two weeks ago, not having any money with which to buy food for the Sabbath, I began to worry. From whence will come my aid? And as I walked along the deserted road I suddenly saw rising before me, right out of the ground, the Evil Spirit himself! 'Why do you look so worried, Hershel?' he asked me.

"'Why should I be jolly?' I replied. 'It's Thursday already and my wife hasn't a broken kopek to go to market with.'

"When the Evil Spirit heard this he laughed. 'What a fool!' he leered at me. 'Why don't you go to the rabbi's house and, when no one is looking, steal from his table a silver spoon so you'll spend a nice Sabbath?'

"So I did as he said. And believe me, I had a pleasant Sabbath! A week ago Thursday I again didn't have anything for the Sabbath. Again I decided to go to the rabbi's house for a silver spoon. But on the way there, I met with the Good Spirit who buttonholed me. 'Where is a Jew going, Hershel?' he asked.

"I cringed. 'I'm on my way to the rabbi's house to steal a silver spoon so that I'll be able to buy food for the Sabbath,' I replied.

"Hearing this, the Good Spirit began to preach at me. 'How can you do such an awful thing, Hershel?' he demanded. 'The

very idea should make you tremble like a leaf! Surely, a man
of your learning knows the difference between good and evil!
It is specifically mentioned in the Ten Commandments: Thou
shall not steal.'

"'Nonsense!' I replied. 'Granted I do know that to steal a
silver spoon from the rabbi is a sin, but what can I do when
the rabbi, who employs me as his jester, doesn't pay me my
weekly wages?'

"'Follow my advice,' said the Good Spirit, 'don't steal and
God will surely come to your aid.'

"Believe me, Rabbi, the Good Spirit stuck to me like a leech
and wouldn't let go of me until I agreed to follow his advice. I
returned to my shanty and observed the Sabbath in the usual
way, may it not be said of my worst enemy, O Lord!

"Now, Rabbi, today is again Thursday and, as usual, I expect
to get no money from you, so my Sabbath will again be
ruined. I walked about racking my poor brains: whose advice
should I follow — that of the Good Spirit, or that of the Evil
Spirit? And, as I was struggling within myself, who should
appear if not the Good Spirit!

"'You see, Hershel!' he cried, triumphantly. 'A man has got to
be honest! You see for yourself how it was possible for you to
celebrate the Sabbath without wicked thievery!'

"'Indeed I did,' I answered him tartly. 'And what a wretched
Sabbath it was too! My family and I were so famished, we
were almost ready to collapse, although it was hardly a hair's
difference from what we usually feel every day in the week.
No, my good brother, rest assured I shan't repeat that mistake
twice. This coming week, praise God, I'll again follow the
Evil Spirit's advice!'

"The Good Spirit almost jumped out of his shoes.

"'Once and for all, Hershel, don't you dare steal!' he cried.

"That, Rabbi, was about the last straw! I was going to show him up, so I said to the Good Spirit, 'If you are such a saint, why don't you go to the Rabbi and tell him he should pay me my wages so I can celebrate God's Sabbath together with all other Jews?' So what do you think the Good Spirit answered?

"'Believe me, Hershel,' he assured me with tears in his eyes. 'Gladly would I do this little favor, but I swear before God that I don't even know the rabbi at all. In fact, I've never even crossed his threshold in all these many years!'"

— *from Ausubel, A Treasury of Jewish Folklore*

Apparently the explicit biblical law that an employer must pay a worker his wages at the end of the day (Lev. 19:13, Deut. 24:15) could be flouted by certain powerful rabbis with impunity. Under these circumstances, Jewish folkore, reflecting popular notions of justice, was even willing to countenance stealing!

For biographical information about Hershel Ostropolier, the most famous (or notorious) of all Jewish *schnorrer*s (impudent beggars), see the endnote to the next story.

⌘⌘⌘

Some townsmen fell to discussing the vexing question of the rich and the poor as they sat around the stove in the House of Study. They exchanged opinions on the inequality of life: while heaven to some, it was hell for others.

"Ah, if men could only live a life of ease, if poverty were abolished from the world!" one of them, a professional mendicant, chimed in.

"Certainly poverty is hell," another seconded him. "Life is confoundedly hard when you haven't got a copper. You listen to me. I know how to remedy this evil. If people would follow my plan, they would put all they own, cash as well as property, into a common fund and then each one would draw upon it according to his needs. Believe me, there would be enough for everyone. Isn't this a fine plan?"

"Indeed it is," they all agreed. "And what have you got to say to this Hershel?" one of them demanded.

"It's a masterly plan, but the question is how to carry it out. I'll tell you what," Hershel suggested to the proponent of the novel idea. "Let's divide the task: I'll undertake to get the endorsement of the poor and you can tackle the rich."
— *from Irving Howe and Eliezer Greenberg,*
A Treasury of Yiddish Stories

Hershel Ostropolier (1770-1810) lived in the Ukraine. For a time, he was actually a jester in the court of a Hasidic *rebbe*. The *rebbe* had Hershel thrown down a flight of stairs for his sarcasm. He sustained injuries that led to his untimely death. Thereafter, legends arose portraying him as an ascerbic wit, who lost no opportunity to lampoon the pious hypocrites, misers and exploiters of the poor within the Jewish community.

⌘⌘⌘

Joha always loved a wedding, even when it couldn't be his own. And Joha also loved food. And what better place to enjoy good food than at a wedding, especially at someone else's expense!

One day, Joha was walking down the street, dressed in his usual ragged clothes, when he passed the large house of a wealthy family and noticed there was a celebration going on.

He asked the guards about the occasion. They told him that a wedding was taking place and the feast was about to begin. When Joha heard the words *wedding* and *feast*, he asked himself, "What better combination could there be? But how is it that I was not invited?" Then he said to himself aloud, with a broad smile, "I will have to see for myself."

Since the poor people of the town were often invited to even the richest of weddings, the guards let Joha through the gates. When Joha knocked on the door of the house, the father of the bride opened the door. Seeing this beggarly looking man, he said, "You are not invited to my daughter's wedding feast."

Joha left. He went to a friend's house and borrowed some very fine clothes, even a high hat. And then he returned to the house of the wedding feast.

The guards greeted him with great courtesy, ushered him to the door of the house and knocked on the door for him. When the father of the bride opened the door and saw this elegantly dressed stranger, he invited him in with great *kovod* (honor) and seated him at the head table. And the father of the bride himself began to bring in the choicest foods and wines to him. Joha watched as the food was placed in front of him. Then he took the meat with the pomegranate seeds and stuffed it all down his sleeves. "Eat, sleeves!" he said with a hearty laugh. He took the other meats and rice and vegetables and salads and crammed them into all of his pockets until they were packed and overflowing with food. "Eat, clothes! Drink, pockets! Enjoy the feast, my clothes!"

The guests stopped eating, stopped drinking, stopped talking! All their eyes were on the stranger, watching this elaborate ritual, bewildered by what they saw. The father of the bride ran over to Joha and shouted, "What are you doing? How dare you do this! Explain yourself!"

And Joha, with a laugh, replied. "Sir, you turned me away
when I came to the door in ragged clothes. But when I returned wearing fine clothes, you invited me in with great
honor. It is clear that you were inviting only my clothes. So
they are eating the feast."

And then Joha, paying no more attention to the host, continued eating. "Eat some more, sleeves! Drink heartily, pockets!"
— from Peninnah Schram, Ed.,
Chosen Tales, Stories Told by Jewish Storytellers

Joha was the counterpart to Hershel Ostropolier among Oriental
(Mizrachi) Jews.

The Disputation

During the Middle Ages, Christian authorities often forced Jews
into publicly "debating" the merits of Judaism before judges con-
sisting of (who else?) the Christian authorities themselves. It was
a form of harassment that could result in anything from public
humiliation to imprisonment, the burning of the Talmud or other
punitive measures. Yet, as the following story illustrates, Jews
managed to find humor even in such a bleak situation.

In a certain town lived a priest who hated the Jews. Once, as
he was passing by the window of a Jewish school, he heard
the children inside studying the verse from Isaiah, "A little
one shall become a thousand, and a small one a strong nation." Stepping inside, he asked the rabbi what that meant.

"It means," said the rabbi, "that one day we will be a great and
mighty nation."

It infuriated the priest that such a lowly and despised people
should dream of being great, and so he went to the king and
accused them of disloyalty.

"What do you suggest we do about it?" asked the king.

"Your Majesty," said the priest, "I suggest you tell the Jews to choose their wisest delegate, and he and I will hold a debate. If I win, you can banish them and confiscate their property."

The king thought this a good idea and ordered it carried out. When news of the decree reached the Jews, they were seized with panic. Not a single one of them was willing to debate the priest, because each feared to be his people's downfall. They called for a public fast and sat in the synagogue saying Psalms and beseeching Providence.

As they were doing this, the town fool passed by the synagogue, stepped inside and asked, "Brothers, why all the weeping and wailing?" When told the reason, he scratched his head, thought a while and said, "Well, if you'd like, I'll go debate with the priest." Hearing him, the Jews thought, "There's no doubt this fellow is the foolishest fool there ever was, but who can think of anyone better? Whatever will be, will be."

And so they agreed to send the fool to the debate. The king had a platform built in the city square, and he and his court sat in front of it while all his subjects, men, women, and children, stood in the rear. Then the priest and the fool mounted the platform and the priest asked the fool, "Shall we agree to talk to each other in sign language?"

"Why not?" said the fool.

So the priest reached into his pocket and took out an egg, and the fool reached into his pocket and took out some salt.

Then the priest raised two fingers, and the fool raised one finger.

Finally, the priest took a handful of barley seeds and scattered them on the ground, and the fool opened up his bag and let out a hen, which proceeded to eat the seeds up.

"Your Majesty," said the priest, turning to the king, "this Jew has answered my questions with such wisdom that I'm afraid he won the debate."

"But tell us, Father," said the uncomprehending king, "what did you ask him and what did he answer?"

"First," said the priest, "I showed him an egg to tell him that the Jews are two-faced: white as an eggshell on the outside, but yellow on the inside. He replied with some salt to say that the Jews are the salt of the earth. Then I raised two fingers: that meant that the Jews serve two deities, God and Mammon. He replied with one finger to say that the Jews worship the single Lord of Heaven and Earth. Finally, I scattered barley seeds on the ground, signifying that the Jews are scattered all over and will never unite again, and he had a hen eat the seeds up to tell me that the Jew's Messiah will gather them together from the four corners of the earth. At that point, I had no choice but to concede defeat."

And so, to the great joy of the Jews, the king's decree was annulled. Then, astonished that the town fool had understood and bested the priest, they asked him to explain how he had done it.

"To tell you the truth," said the fool, "that priest must be out of his mind. Right away he got angry and made as if to throw an egg at me, so I took out some salt and made as if to rub it in his eyes. 'Oh! Ho!' he says sticking up two fingers at me, 'I'll poke out both your eyes!' 'Just try it,' I say, sticking up my finger at him, 'and I'll ram this down your throat!' That made him so mad that he took some perfectly good barley and

began throwing it on the ground. Well, I wasn't going to let it
go to waste, so I let my hen eat it. Wouldn't you have done
the same if it was your hen?"
— *from Jewish Folktales, selected and retold by Pinhas Sadeh*

Dying to Get In

Eleazer Bokar appeared at the gates of Heaven and knocked
for admittance. The great doors slowly swung open and the
patriarch Abraham stepped out blowing his golden trumpet.
When he finished the welcoming concerto, he addressed
Eleazer:

"Greetings, blood of my blood and flesh of my flesh. Jehovah
awaits you."

Eleazar stepped forward to enter the celestial portals, but
patriarch Abraham halted him with an imperious upflung
palm. "Wait, my brother! Before you enter Jehovah's kingdom, you must be worthy of the honor."

"How can I prove my worthiness?"

"You must show that, at least once in your mortal life, you
displayed outstanding courage. Can you recall one unques-
tionably brave deed?"

Eleazer's face brightened. "Yes, I can. I remember once I
went to the Roman Consul's palace and I met him face to
face. He was surrounded by dozens of legionnaires, all of
them armed to the teeth, but I simply ignored them. I told him
he was a camel's ass, a vulture feeding on the bones of
Jerusalem's oppressed people and a persecutor of the Jews.
Then I spat in his face."

Abraham was immensely impressed. "I must agree, that was
an extremely brave thing to do considering all the armed

guards who were present, and knowing the Roman Consul's hatred for the Jews. Yes, my brother, you certainly have earned admittance into Paradise, but tell me, when did all this happen?"

"Oh," replied Eleazer casually, "about three or four minutes ago."
— *from Henry Spaulding, Ed., Encyclopedia of Jewish Humor*

Gratitude for Small Favors (or He Got Off Easy)

Emperor Hadrian, on his way to war, rode past a garden where he observed a very old man planting a fig tree. He halted his horse and asked: "Why in your old age do you labor so zealously? Do you expect to eat the fruit of the tree you are planting?''

The old man replied; "If it be the will of God, I shall eat of it; if not, my sons will enjoy it."

Three years later the Emperor passed the garden again. The same old man approached Hadrian with a basket of figs, and, handing it to him, said: "My master, be good enough to receive this gift. I am the man to whom you spoke three years ago."

The Emperor was touched, and commanded that the basket be filled with gold pieces and returned to the diligent old man.

The wife of a neighbor chanced to be in the gray-beard's home when he returned with the gold. She heard his story and immediately commanded her husband to take the Emperor a large basket filled with varied fruits. "He loves the fruit of this region," she said, "and he may, as a reward, fill your basket with gold pieces."

Her husband followed her advice and bringing the fruit to the Emperor, said: "Sire, I have heard that you are fond of fruit, and I have brought these for your enjoyment."

On hearing the whole story, the Emperor became incensed at the man's impudence and gave orders to his soldiery to throw the fruit at his face. Bruised and half-blinded, the schemer returned to his home.

"How did you fare?" asked his wife greedily.

"I fared excellently," replied her husband. "Had I taken citrons, I would have died of the blows" (*Midrash, Leviticus Rabbah 25*).
                   — *from Newman and Spitz, The Talmudic Anthology*

A Lesson in Hospitality

Jacob Krantz, the great *maggid* (preacher) of Dubno (1740-1804), was famed for his parables. Arriving in a certain town one day, he stopped at the house of a rich man.

"Peace to you!" the host greeted him. "Sit down and tell me a good parable."

"With pleasure," replied the preacher. "A poor man once brought home a goat he had purchased at the fair, and his wife immediately began to try to milk it. Of course she could not get a drop. 'Pooh!' she cried. 'This animal cannot be a goat. There is no milk in her.' To which her husband replied: 'You are wrong, my beloved. It is a goat, and there is milk in her. But she has come a long distance and is tired and hungry and thirsty. Supply her needs, and let her rest overnight, and you will see, tomorrow she will give plenty of milk.'"
                   — *from Browne, The Wisdom of Israel*

Chutzpa

Chutzpa is one Jewish characteristic that is exclusively secular. The religious authorities universally condemn it because it defies accepted standards of propriety. That, of course, is its subversive appeal.

A group of young miscreants were caught red-handed break-ing the Sabbath peace. They were smoking, playing cards and doing other things forbidden on the Sabbath.

On the following day, when they were brought up on charges before the rabbi, he sternly demanded an explanation of them.

The first said: "Rabbi, I was absent-minded; I forgot that it was the Sabbath."

"That could be," said the rabbi, stroking his beard reflectively. "You are forgiven!"

The second said: "I also was absent-minded; I forgot that one musn't gamble on the Sabbath."

"That could be," said the rabbi, stroking is beard reflectively. "You are forgiven!"

Then the turn came for the owner of the house in which the young men had been found desecrating the Sabbath.

"And what is your excuse?" asked the rabbi. "Were you absent-minded too?"

"Indeed I was, Rabbi," answered the man regretfully.

"What did you forget?"

"I forgot to pull the curtains down!" said the man.
                              — *from Ausubel, A Treasury of Jewish Folklore*

⌘⌘⌘

On the fast day of Tisha B'Av, a sick Jew went to see the rabbi in order to get his permission to eat, for he was afraid his health would suffer if he didn't. But, as he entered the rabbi's house, he was struck dumb with amazement when he saw the rabbi enjoying a hearty lunch.

"Rabbi," he faltered, not at all sure of himself, "I'm a sick man. dD I have to fast today?"

"What a question!" replied the rabbi, his mouth full of roast duck. "Of course you do!"

For a moment the petitioner stood in bewilderment, not knowing whether he was coming or going. Finally, he scraped up sufficient courage to ask, "Pardon my impertinence, Rabbi, but how can you order me to fast when you yourself are eating?"

"I wasn't fool enough to ask the rabbi," replied the rabbi with a grin and went on with his lunch.
                              — *from Ausubel, A Treasury of Jewish Folklore*

Among devout Jews, Tisha B'Av is the most solemn Jewish holiday. It commemorates the destruction of the First and Second Temple. In addition to fasting, worshipers sit on the floor or on low benches in a darkened synagogue and read from the Book of Lamentations.

⌘⌘⌘

As the rabbi sat deep in thought, a youth came before him and said: "Rabbi, I want to confess. I'm guilty of a great sin. I failed to say grace one day last month."

"Tsk-tsk!" murmured the Rabbi. "How can any Jew eat without saying grace?"

"How could I say grace, Rabbi, when I hadn't washed my hands?"

"*Oy vey!*" wailed the Rabbi. "How can a Jew swallow a mouthful without first washing his hands?"

"But you see, Rabbi, the food was not kosher."

"Not kosher! How can a Jew eat food that's not kosher?"

"But Rabbi, how in the world could it be kosher; it was in the house of a Gentile?"

What! You miserable apostate! How could you eat in the house of a Gentile?"

"But Rabbi, no Jew was willing to feed me!"

"That's a wicked lie!" cried the Rabbi. "Who has ever heard of a Jew refusing food to anybody who is hungry?"

"But Rabbi," argued the youth, "it was Yom Kippur!"
— *from Ausubel, A Treasury of Jewish Folklore*

Sometimes it's better not to ask too many questions. So why does a Jew always answer a question with a question? Why not?

Chapter VII.
Women

There is a great deal of misogyny in Jewish tradition, as is true for other patriarchies, but these stories reflect a very different approach.

> It once happened that a pious man married a pious woman, and they did not produce children. They said, "We are of no use to the Holy One, Blessed be He," and they arose and divorced each other. The man went and married a wicked woman, and she made him wicked, while the woman went and married a wicked man, and she made him righteous. This proves that all depends on the woman (*Midrash, Genesis Rabbah 17:7*).
>
> — *from Telushkin, Jewish Wisdom.*

Lilith, the First Feminist

How lonely Adam was that first day as he watched the animals parade by, two by two, with a companion. And God took pity on him and made him a partner, scooping out another handful of dust from the earth. This creature was named Lilith and she became Adam's wife.

Because this first woman was equal to Adam in every way, having been made by God out of the same earth and on the same day as her husband, she insisted on enjoying equal footing with him in the Garden: sharing the labor and its reward, working side by side to tend the growing things entrusted to their care.

Also in the ways of love between a man and a woman, Lilith wished to share equally, sometimes lying on top of her lover and sometimes below him. For were they not full partners in creation?

But this was too much for Adam to bear, and he complained to God, saying, "Is this why I have been created, to share *everything* with her? When I asked for a companion, I did not mean this!"

When Lilith heard Adam's complaint, she decided to leave the Garden, where she was not welcome, and make a new home for herself far away. Pronouncing the Awesome Name, she flew away to the shores of the Sea of Reeds.

Instantly Adam was sorry that he had driven her away, and he once more cried out to God, "My wife has deserted me! Again, I am all alone!"

So God sent three angels, Senoy, Sansenoyk and Semangelof, to fetch Lilith back to Eden. But she was not willing to return, for she knew that Adam did not desire her the way she was.

"If you do not return with us," threatened the angels, "you will lose one hundred of your children each day until you change your mind."

"So be it," replied Lilith. And she sent them back to Eden empty-handed.

From that day on, in revenge for her hurt pride and slaughtered children, Lilith has prowled through the night, looking for newborn babies to harm. With her long black hair and great flapping wings, she will sometimes swoop down on day-old baby boys or on baby girls during their first twenty days of life and suck the breath out of them.

But at heart she is not cruel. For out of compassion for her
sister creatures, she has betrayed her own power: "If you
inscribe the names of the three angels, Senoy, Sansenoy, and
Semangelof, in an amulet and tie this charm around your
children's neck," she has whispered to the mothers of these
innocent babies, "I promise not to harm even one hair on their
heads."

And she has never failed to keep her word.
        — *from Frankel, The Classic Tales, 4000 Years of Jewish*
                                                                Lore

Before the emergence of the feminist movement, Lilith was typically depicted as a demon without any redeeming qualities. There
is a Jewish feminist journal entitled *Lilith*. Surprised?

Leah Turns the Tables on Jacob

In the Bible, Jacob is tricked into marrying Laban's oldest daughter, Leah, instead of the daughter he loved, Rachel. Leah was
obviously part of this deception. Here, in the following legend,
Leah defends her conduct by reminding Jacob that he practiced a
similar deception on his father, Isaac, in order to receive the blessing that should have gone to his older brother, Esau.

When the bride was led into the nuptial chamber, the guests extin-
guished all the candles, much to Jacob's amazement. But their
explanation satisfied him. "Did you think," they said, "we have as
little sense of decency as your countrymen?" Jacob therefore did
not discover the deception practiced upon him until morning.
During the night Leah responded whenever he called Rachel, for
which he reproached her bitterly when daylight came. "Oh you
deceiver, daughter of a deceiver, why did you answer me when I
called Rachel's name?" "Is there a teacher without a pupil?" asked
Leah, in return. "I but profited by your instruction. When your
father called you Esau, did you not say, 'Here am I?'"
        — *adapted from Ginzberg, Legends of the Bible*

In other words, what goes around, comes around.

A Rabbinical Sage Learns the Law from His Wife

There were some criminals in Rabbi Meir's neighborhood who caused him much trouble, and he prayed that they should die. His wife Beruriah said to him: "What are you thinking? [*i.e.*, How could you possibly believe that such a prayer is even allowed?] Do you justify it on the basis of the verse [in Psalms 104:35], 'May sinners disappear from the earth, and the wicked be no more?' But the word that you take to mean 'sinners' [Hebrew: *hot-tim*] can also be read as 'sins' [*hatta-im*]; in other words, 'Let sins disappear from the earth.' Furthermore, look at the end of the verse, 'and the wicked be no more.' Once the sins will cease, they will no longer be wicked men! Rather pray that they repent, and there will be no more wicked people around." Rabbi Meir did pray for them, and the criminals repented (*Berakhot 10a*).

— from Telushkin, Jewish Wisdom

Beruriah (second century C.E.) is the only woman in the entire Talmud who is credited with teaching the law to a man. Her intellectual abilities apparently aroused some resentment among the rabbis. According to rabbinic lore, she suffered from many misfortunes during her life. The great Bible and Talmud scholar, Rashi (an acronym for Rabbi Solomon Yitzhak ben Isaac) who lived in France from 1040 to 1105 C.E., even claimed she came to a bad end after being seduced by one of her husband's students.

Take Your Choice: Wealth, Learning, or a Virtuous Woman

There once lived a man who owned a beautiful spice garden. When the time came for him to die, he called his three sons and said to them, "Promise me that you will never quarrel but will always love one another. And promise to guard our spice garden from thieves, for it is my most precious possession."

And the sons swore to do what their father had asked.

After the father died, the sons agreed to take turns watching over the garden. On the first night Elijah appeared before the oldest son and asked him, "Would you rather have wealth, learning or a virtuous wife?" he asked.

The son replied, "I would rather have wealth."

So Elijah gave him a gold coin, and he became rich.

The next night Elijah appeared before the second son. "Would you rather have wealth, learning or a virtuous wife?" he asked.

The second son said, "I would rather have learning."

So Elijah handed him a book, and at once he knew the whole Torah.

On the third night Elijah appeared before the youngest son. "Would you rather have wealth, learning or a virtuous wife?" he asked him.

"I would rather marry a virtuous woman," replied the youngest son, "for her price is above rubies."

"Then you must come with me," said Elijah.

The next day they journeyed to a town [in search of a virtuous woman to become the youngest son's wife] and stayed at an inn. That night Elijah overheard the geese and the chickens saying, "What a sinner this young man must be to deserve such a wicked wife! For the people here are evildoers and idolaters." [Apparently, the animals have the power to discern

the character of unmarried women and Elijah understands
their language!]

The next day they traveled to a second inn. Again Elijah
overheard the geese and chickens saying, "How sinful this
young man must be to deserve such a wretch for a wife, for
the people here are heartless and without faith."

The third day they traveled to another inn. That night Elijah
overheard the geese and chickens saying, "He must be a
virtuous young man to merit such a worthy bride! For the
family here is pious and full of kind deeds!"

So Elijah became the *shadkhan* (matchmaker) and arranged
for the two young people to be married.

Years later Elijah disguised himself as a beggar and returned
to see what had happened to the three sons. When he came to
the house of the oldest son, he was not admitted, for the son
had become a heartless miser and shared none of his wealth
with the poor.

Elijah appeared before him and said, "I gave you wealth, but
you have proved unworthy of it." And he took back the gold
coin, and the man lost all he had.

He next went to the house of the second son to whom he had
given learning. But his son had grown arrogant because of his
great knowledge and held himself above all others. Elijah took
back the book, and he forgot all he knew.

Then he came to the house of the youngest son. His wife
welcomed him graciously into the house and fed him the
finest foods on her best dishes. When her husband returned,
Elijah said to him, "Because of the merits of your wife, I am
giving you wealth and learning, for the two of you will make

good use of them." And so the youngest son's wish for a
virtuous wife proved a true blessing.

> — *from Frankel, The Classic Tales,*
> *4000 Years of Jewish Lore*

This Elijah story clearly gives the wife full credit for earning the
blessings of wealth and learning for herself and her husband. But
women who are neither wives nor mothers rarely receive any rec-
ognition in traditional literature. The "woman of valor" whose "price
is above rubies," celebrated in Proverbs 31:10-31, is really a mis-
translation for "a capable wife."

Heroism and Sacrifice

"Once," King Solomon related, "there was a loving couple
who lived happily and lacked for nothing. One day the husband came into possession of some fine merchandise, and
though he could have sold it for a large profit in the capital, he
did not go there, being loath to leave his wife alone. Yet the
woman, sensing that her husband was unhappy, asked him for
the reason, and, when told it, urged him to make the trip at
once. And so he listened to her and set out, only to be arrested
by the king upon reaching the capital and thrown into prison.
The woman waited and waited for him, and when at last she
found out what had happened, she put on her best clothes and
went to the king's court to ask for her husband back. The king
and his grand vizier replied that they would grant her wish on
the condition that she lie with them both. And so it was agreed
that they would come to her lodgings the next day.

"The woman returned to her lodgings, removed the rugs from
the floor, and smeared glue all over it. When the king and his
grand vizier came the next day, they slipped as they entered
the room and stuck to the floor. The woman locked the door
and told them, "If you want to be freed, you yourselves had
better free all your prisoners." The king begged in vain to be
allowed to free only the woman's husband, but, in the end, he

had to promise her what she asked for and put it in writing, stamped with the royal seal. The next day, she went and stood by the prison gates in order to see the prisoners freed. A huge throng of them, some thirty thousand men, were liberated from bondage, and among the last to emerge was her husband. And so you see what a woman's word and devotion are worth."

— adapted from Jewish Folktales,
selected and retold by Pinhas Sadeh

One might expect that a virtuous Jewish woman would seek to thwart evil men who demand sexual favors from her. However, her insistence that the king free not just her husband but all the prisoners is an extraordinary act of conscience. (She also should go down in history as the inventor of "crazy glue," but that is another matter.)

It is rare to find any story in biblical literature in which a woman is shown to take action that transcends the welfare of her immediate family. The few examples include the Hebrew midwives from Exodus, Shifra and Puah, who saved the lives of firstborn Hebrew boys; Pharoah's daughter, who saved the baby Moses; Deborah, the judge; and Esther, although she had to be prodded by Mordecai. Judith appears in a book from the Apocrypha as an avenger against a foreign enemy.

Jewish feminists searching for heroines have adopted Moses' sister, Miriam, but her great claim to fame is rejoicing over the drowning of the Egyptian soldiers in the Red Sea. The only time she dared to criticize Moses, she was afflicted with leprosy for seven days. Aaron, her other brother, made the same complaint against Moses and went unpunished (*Numbers 11:31-34*).

The Talmud, which often humanizes the harsh legal code of the Bible, is in some ways more repressive when it comes to the status of women. Except for Beruriah, Rabbi Meir's wife, the Talmud is devoid of any women who think for themselves.

The Story of Susanna

There once lived in Babylon a man named Joakim. He married a wife named Susanna, the daughter of Hilkiah, a very beautiful and pious woman. Her parents also were upright people and instructed their daughter in the Law of Moses. Joakim was very rich, and he had a fine garden adjoining his house and the Jews used to come to visit him because he was the most distinguished of them all.

That year two of the elders of the people were appointed judges, men of the kind of whom the Lord said, "Lawlessness came forth from Babylon, from elders who were judges, who were supposed to guide the people."

These men came constantly to Joakim's house, and all who had cases to be decided came to them there. And it happened that when the people left at midday, Susanna would go into her husband's garden and walk about. So the two elders saw her every day and they conceived a passion for her. They were both smitten with her, but they could not disclose their feelings to each other, for they were ashamed to reveal their passion, and they watched jealously every day for a sight of her. And they said to one another, "Let us go home, for it is dinner-time."

So they went out of the garden and parted; then they turned back and encountered one another. And when they questioned one another as to the explanation, they admitted their passion. Then they agreed together upon a time when they would be able to find her alone.

Now it happened, as they were watching for an opportunity, that she went in one day as usual with no one but her two maids and wished to bathe, as it was very hot. And there was no one there except the two elders who had hidden themselves and were watching her. And she said to her maids, "Bring me olive oil and soap, and close the doors of the garden so that I can bathe."

And they did as she told them and shut the doors of the garden and went out at the side doors to bring what they had been ordered to bring, and they did not see the elders for they were hidden. And when the maids went out, the two elders got up and ran to her and said, "Here the doors of the garden are shut, and no one can see us, and we are in love with you, so give your consent and lie with us. If you do not, we will testify against you that there was a young man with you, and that was why you dismissed your maids."

And Susanna groaned and said, "I am in a tight place. For if I do this, it means my end; but if I refuse, I cannot escape your plot. I had rather not do it and fall into your hands than commit sin in the Lord's sight!"

Then Susanna gave a loud scream, and the two elders shouted against her. And one of them ran and opened the garden doors. And when the people in the house heard the shouting in the garden, they rushed through the side doors to see what had happened to her. And when the elders told their story, her maids were deeply ashamed, for such a thing had never been said about Susanna.

The next day the elders came, full of their wicked design to put Susanna to death. And they said before the people who gathered together, "Send for Susanna, the daughter of Hilkiah, Joakim's wife."

And they did so. And she came, with her parents and her children and all her relatives.

And the two elders stood up in the midst of the people and laid their hands on her head, and she wept and looked up to heaven, for her heart trusted in the Lord. And the elders said, "As we were walking by ourselves in the garden, this woman came in with two maids and shut the doors of the garden and dismissed her maids, and a young man, who had been hidden, came to her and lay down with her. And we were in the corner of the garden, and when we saw this wicked action, we ran up to them, and though we saw them together, we could not hold him because he was stronger than we and opened the doors and rushed out. But we laid hold of this woman and asked her who the young man was; and she would not tell us. This is our testimony."

The assembly believed them, as they were elders of the people and judges, and they condemned her to death. But Susanna uttered a loud cry, and said, "Eternal God, you who know what is hidden, who know all things before they happen, you know that what they have testified to is false, and here I am to die when I have done none of the things they have so wickedly charged me with."

And the Lord heard her cry, and as she was being led away to be put to death, God stirred up the holy spirit of a young man named Daniel, and he loudly shouted, "I am clear of the blood of this woman."

And the people turned to him and said, "What does this mean?"

And he took his stand in the midst of them and said, "Are you such fools, you Israelites, that you have condemned a daughter of Israel without any examination or ascertaining the truth? Go back to the place of trial. For these men have borne false witness against her."

So the people hurried back. And Daniel said to them, "Separate the witnesses from one another, and I will examine them."

And when they were separated, he called one of them to him and said, "You old man of wickedness, your former sins have caught up with you! The Lord said 'You shall not put an innocent and upright man to death,' yet you made unjust decisions, condemning the innocent and acquitting the guilty. So now, if you saw this woman, tell us, under which tree did you meet them?"

He answered, "Under a mastic tree" [a small shrub].

And he had him removed and ordered them to bring in the other. And he said to him, "You descendant of Canaan and not of Judah, beauty has beguiled you, and desire has corrupted your heart! This is how you have been treating the daughters of Israel, and they yielded to you through fear, but a daughter of Judah would not endure your wickedness. So now tell me, under which tree did you catch them embracing each other?"

And he said, "Under an oak tree."

And the whole company uttered a great shout and threw themselves upon the two elders, for Daniel had convicted them out of their own mouths of having borne false witness, and treated them as they had wickedly planned to treat their neighbor. They obeyed the Law of Moses and killed them. And innocent blood was saved that day.

And Hilkiah and his wife praised God for their daughter Susanna and so did Joakim her husband and all her relatives, because she had done nothing immodest. And from that day onward, Daniel had a great reputation in the eyes of the people.
— *adapted from The Apocrypha, trans. by Edgar J. Goodspeed*

The Daniel depicted in this story is none other than the biblical hero. Here he appears in the Apocrypha, a non-biblical Jewish source.

It is impossible to overlook the fact that this story is marred by prejudicial attitudes toward non-Jews (Canaanites) and a different branch of Jews (Israelites). Furthermore, the punishment meted out to the elders appears unduly harsh, as is generally the case with biblical law. Yet, the story has great merit because it teaches that the claims of the ruling elite should be carefully scrutinized and that all people, including women, are entitled to equal justice under the law. For that reason, this story could just as easily belong in Chapter II, "Confronting Injustice."

Wisdom Before Beauty

Long ago in the city of Constantinople there lived a girl, the only child of a great rabbi, whose face resembled that of a wild beast. But even though she was very ugly, she was also very wise, the wisest person in all of Constantinople. Yet because of her great ugliness, her parents kept her locked away in the attic above the House of Study. She received her food through a small opening in the door, and she passed through that same opening whatever she wished to send away. But her face was never seen.

Once a youth from a distant country came to Constantinople to study. He first went to the House of Study and there heard the rabbi present a question that none of the students could answer. All day the youth pondered the rabbi's question, but he was unable to discover the answer. Finally, exhausted from his efforts, he left the House of Study to walk about the city.

When he returned a few hours later, he found a slip of paper lying on his open book. When he read the words written on the slip, he knew at once that here was the answer to the rabbi's question. But when he asked the other students which of them had put the slip of paper there, they only laughed at him.

"Why are you laughing?" he asked them.

"The person who wrote the answer to the rabbi's question is his daughter," they replied. "She lives in the attic above this room. Whenever her father asks a question that is too difficult for us, she always writes it down on a slip of paper and drops it through the floorboards. There is no one wiser in the whole city."

When the youth heard of this extraordinary girl, he wished to make her his wife. But the others warned him not to pursue the matter further.

"For she is a cursed creature whom no one may look upon because of her ugliness. Her father will never give his consent."

Yet the youth would not be dissuaded. "Such wisdom cannot live in an ugly vessel!" he insisted.

As the other students had predicted, the girl's father at first refused to give his consent to the marriage. The youth persisted, however, until finally the rabbi relented and agreed to permit his only daughter to marry.
— *from Frankel, The Classic Tales, 4000 Years of Jewish Lore*

This story sounds like a variation on the Beauty and the Beast theme and is likely common to a number of cultures.

You've Come a Long Way, Skotsl

You know that among Yiddish speakers, the expression *Skotsl kumt* [Skotsl's here] is used by women to greet another woman when she comes into the house. Would you like to know its origin? I'll tell you a story that will explain it.

Once upon a time the women complained that everything in the world belonged to men. Men got to perform the *mitsvas* [the religious commandments]; they got to read from the Torah. In short, they got to do everything. As for the women, they got nothing. No one paid them any attention at all. So they decided to form a deputation that would take their complaint to the Lord of the Universe.

But how was it to be done? Well, they decided that they would heap women up in a pile, one on top of the other, until the woman at the very tip could pull herself into heaven. At the top of the pile was Skotsl. Because she was both very clever and a skillful speaker, she was chosen as the one to talk with the Lord of the Universe.

Everything went well as the women were climbing onto each other. But just as Skotsl reached the top, the hunchbacked woman at the base of the pile twisted about, and the women came tumbling down. Well, of course there was nothing but noise and confusion, with everyone trying to locate everyone else. But Skotsl was nowhere to be found, though they searched for her everywhere. And so there was no one who could be counted on to talk with God, and the situation of the women remained unchanged. Everything still belonged to the men.

But from that time on, women have not lost their hope that one day Skotsl will come. And that's why, whenever a woman comes into a house, they call out joyfully, "*Skotsl kumt* (Here comes Skotsl)," because who knows, one day she might really be there.

— from Weinreich, Ed., Yiddish Folktales

That *Skotsl* has finally come is a tribute to feminists, including Jewish ones such as Ernestine Rose, Emma Goldman, Bella Abzug, Betty Friedan and Gloria Steinhem (half-Jewish). In Jewish life, the Conservative, Reconstructionist and Reform movements now ordain female rabbis and most of their congregations are egalitarian. Even among the Orthodox, women like Blu

Greenberg are demanding greater equality for women. The Secular Humanistic Jewish movement has practiced gender equality for decades.

The Light Side: The Rabbi and the *Rebbitzen*

Once there was a young rabbi, but he was a great *shlemiel* and never got anywhere despite his learning.

One day, a new rabbi was being chosen for the principal synagogue in town. Our *shlemiel*, too, was a candidate for the post.

"Since you are such a *shlemiel* leave the whole matter to me!" his wife told him. So he let her do all the wirepulling and soliciting of influential votes for him.

Finally, with his wife's and God's help, he was elected to the post.

His new dignity turned the rabbi's head. He began to speak grandly to his wife and tried to lay down the law for her in everything. Finally they quarreled.

"To the whole town you may be the rabbi of the Great Synagogue," she lashed out at him, "but to me you're only the same old *shlemiel*! You think that because you're the *rebbe*, I'm the *rebbitzen*. Believe me, it's the other way around. Everybody in town, except you, knows that you're the *rebbe* because I'm the *rebbitzen*!"

— from Ausubel, A Treasury of Jewish Folklore

Chapter VIII.
Jewish-Gentile Relations

There is much in Jewish tradition that conveys hostility and contempt for Gentiles. This attitude was in large part an unfortunate
reaction to anti-Jewish persecutions. The following stories reflect
a different part of the tradition, one that teaches respect.

Abraham and the Heathen

Once, as the Patriarch Abraham sat at the entrance of his tent,
he saw an old tired man approach. Abraham arose and ran
forward to bid him welcome. He begged him to enter his tent
and rest, but the old man declined the invitation and said, "No,
thank you! I will take my rest under a tree."

But, after Abraham continued to press him with his hospitable
attentions the old man allowed himself to be persuaded and
entered the tent.

Abraham placed before him goat's milk and butter and baked
for him fresh cakes. The stranger ate until he was satisfied.
Then Abraham said to him, "Now praise the Lord, the God of
Heaven and earth, Who gives bread to all His creatures."

"I do not know your God," replied the old man coldly. "I will
only praise the god that my hands have fashioned!"

Then Abraham spoke to the old man, told him of God's greatness and loving kindness. He tried to convince him that his idols were senseless things that could neither help nor save anyone. He urged him therefore to abandon them and put his faith in the one true God and thank Him for His gracious acts that He did for him every day. But to all of Abraham's fervent pleas the old man answered indignantly, "How dare you talk to me this way, trying to turn me away from my gods! You and I have nothing in common, so do not impose on me any further with your words, because I will not heed them!"

At this Abraham grew very angry and cried out, "Old man, leave my tent!"

Without a word the old man departed and he was swallowed up by the dark night and the desert.

When the Almighty saw this, He grew very wrathful and appeared before Abraham.

"Where is the man who came to you this night?" He asked sternly.

"The old man was stubborn," replied Abraham. "I tried to persuade him that if he believed in You everything would be well with him. He refused to heed my words so I grew angry and drove him out of my tent."

Then spoke God: "Have you considered what you have done? Reflect for one moment: Here am I, the God of all Creation, and yet have I endured the unbelief of this old man for so many years. I clothed and fed him and supplied all his needs. But when he came to you for just one night you dispensed with all duties of hospitality and compassion and drove him into the wilderness!"

Then Abraham fell upon his face and prayed to God that He
forgive him his sin.

"I will not forgive you," said God, "unless you first ask
forgiveness from the heathen to whom you have done evil!"

Swiftly, Abraham ran out of his tent and into the desert and
after much searching found the old man. Then he fell at his
feet and wept and begged for his forgiveness. The old man
was moved by Abraham's pleas and he forgave him.
                    — from Ausubel, A Treasury of Jewish Folklore

The origins of this story are completely unknown. It stands in complete contrast to the Bible, where worship of pagan gods is considered the worst of all sins. Benjamin Franklin is said to have
once used it in a speech. I consider it a wonderful parable about
the need to respect religious pluralism.

Ishmael, the Disfavored Son, Is Judged to Be Righteous

*"What aileth thee, Hagar? Fear not; for God hath heard
the voice of the lad where he is" (Gen. 21:17).*

Rabbi Isaac said:
> Man is judged only by his deeds at the moment of
> judgment; for it is said of Ishmael: "For God hath
> heard the voice of the lad where he is."

Rabbi Simon said:
> The ministering angels leaped to denounce Ishmael.
> They said to God: Master of the universe, do you
> cause a well to spring for a man whose children are
> destined to make your children die of thirst?
> He said to them: What is he now, righteous or
> wicked?

They said to him: Righteous.
He said to them: I judge a man only by his deeds at
the moment of his judgment. "Arise, lift up the lad.
... And God opened her eyes and she saw a well of
water; and she went, and filled the bottle with
water, and gave the lad drink" (Gen. 21:18-19).
—from Nahum N. Glatzer, Ed.,
Hammer on the Rock, A Short Midrash Reader

Ishmael, Abraham's son from Sarah's handmaiden Hagar, is considered by Arabs to be their first ancestor. In Genesis, Sarah, with God's approval and Abraham's acquiescence, threw him and his mother out of their house, but God took mercy and promised Hagar that Ishmael would be the founder of a great nation. Abraham and Sarah's son, Isaac, reunites with his brother, Ishmael to bury their father. One of the organizations in Israel that work for Jewish-Arab reconciliation is called "The Abraham Fund."

A Midrash on Racism

Once Eleazar ben Simon, returning from his teacher in Migdal
Gedor, was riding his donkey along the shore. As he rode, he
said to himself, "What a great scholar am I! How much Torah
have I acquired!"

Soon he met a tall black man who greeted him, saying, "Peace
to you, O master!"

Eleazar did not return his greeting but instead insulted the
man: "Tell me, wretch, are all the people in your town as
black as you?"

"I don't know," replied the man. "Why don't you ask the
artisan who fashioned me why he made such a shoddy piece
of work?"

The man's strange reply pierced Eleazar's heart, and he realized that he had sinned in speaking this way to him. At once he dismounted from the donkey and asked the man's forgiveness.

"I cannot forgive you until you go to the artisan and ask him to explain why he made me this way," replied the man, and he turned round and began walking toward the town. Eleazar followed him.

When the people saw that it was Rabbi Eleazar who had arrived in their midst, they cried, "Peace unto you, master and teacher!" For Eleazar was known throughout the land as a great sage.

"Whom are you calling master and teacher?" demanded the black man.

"Don't you know that this man is a great rabbi?" asked the people.

"May there be no more such great men in Israel!" said the black man, and he told them what had happened between them on the road into town.

"We beg you to forgive him," the people pleaded with him, "for he is indeed a revered teacher of Torah."

"For your sakes, I will forgive him," answered the black man, "but in the future let him be warned not to behave this way toward his fellow man."

Then Rabbi Eleazar went to the House of Study and taught, "One should always be soft like a reed, not hard like a cedar." For he realized that pride could harden a man's heart and make of his learning a worthless thing.

Then he went to find the stranger to beg his forgiveness, once
again, but the man had vanished. Only then did he realize that
the man had been none other than Elijah the Prophet.
   —*from Frankel, The Classic Tales, 4000 Years of Jewish Lore*

In this story, Elijah teaches the same moral lesson as Martin Luther
King: people deserve to be judged by the content of their character, not the color of their skin.

A Jew Comes to the Aid of a Roman

Rabbi Eleazar ben Shammua was walking along the sea shore
one stormy day when he spied a ship out at sea, which had
fallen into distress and had sunk with all its passengers. Then
he saw a survivor clinging to a plank in the water. The man
rode the waves with the help of the plank and was lifted from
one wave until the next until he came near to the shore. But
the man had been stripped of all his clothes so he remained in
the water to cover his nakedness. Then seeing some pilgrims
on their way to Jerusalem the shipwrecked man called out, "I
am a descendant of Esau your brother. I was caught in a storm
out at sea and all my clothes were pulled off me by the strong
current. Now I beg you to bring me a cloak; anything with
which to cover my nakedness!"

But the people jeered at him and said, "may all your people
end up with the same fate!"

Then the man spied Rabbi Eleazar ben Shammua and called
out to him, "You look to be an honorable sage who cares for
human dignity. See I have been stripped of my clothing and I
beg you to fetch me something to cover my nakedness that I
may come out of the water."

Now Rabbi Eleazar was clothed with seven beautiful robes,
which he had donned to honor his visit to Jerusalem. He took
off one of them, waded in the water and handed it to the

Roman. Then he brought the man home and gave him food and drink as well as two hundred dinars. Finally he escorted him fourteen miles in the direction of his destination.

In the course of a few years, the Roman emperor died and that man who survived the storm was hailed as the new ruler. One of the first things he did was to issue a decree against the inhabitants of the town, whose citizens had treated him so mercilessly. The men were to be executed and the women taken prisoners. In desperation the people sent for Eleazar ben Shammua to go and intercede for them before the new emperor. "You know," he said to them, "that the Romans never do anything without payment."

They told him, "We have four thousand dinars in the communal chest. Here take it and see what you can do to save our lives!"

Rabbi Eleazar took the money and made his way to the royal residence. On his arrival, he sent word to the emperor that a rabbi seeks an audience with him. When he entered the royal chamber, the Roman ruler ran towards him and fell on his face before him. "Sir! What brings you here?" he asked with some amazement.

"I came to intercede with you for that town." said Eleazar.

"Does your Torah contain anything which is a lie?" asked the emperor.

"Of course not," said the rabbi.

Then the emperor went on, "Your Torah teaches: *An Ammonite or a Moabite shall not enter into the assembly of the Lord ... because they met you not with bread and with water in the way (Deut. 23:4-5).*

"and it also says: *Thou shalt not abhor an Edomite, for he is thy brother (Ibid., 8).*

"Now am I not a descendant of Esau your brother? Yet these people showed me no charity, and in disobeying their Torah they incurred the penalty of death."

Rabbi Eleazar nevertheless pleaded urgently. "Forgive them and show them mercy!"

The emperor said to the rabbi, "You know that my government will do no favors without some payment in exchange."

The rabbi quickly replied, "But I have brought four thousand dinars, which I beg you to take and show mercy to these people."

The emperor took the four thousand dinars and said, "Here I give you all this money as a gift to you personally in repayment of the two hundred dinars you gave to me. I also pardon the people of the town, not because they deserve it but only because of your own charity in bringing me into your house and offering me food and drink. Further, you may go to my royal wardrobe and take for yourself seven robes to replace the one you gave to me. Then you may depart in peace and return to your own people."

In telling that story the sages would often quote the verse, *Cast thy bread upon the waters for thou shalt find it after many days (Ecc. 11:1).*

> — *from Bialik and Ravnitzky, Stories of the Sages, from Sefer Ha-Aggadah, selected by Chaim Pearl.*

The real Edomites were a Semitic people with a history of conflict with the ancient Hebrews. They were conquered by John Hyrcanus, a Hasmonean king descended from the Maccabees,

during the late second century B.C.E. They were forcibly converted to Judaism, but became loyal Jews nevertheless and joined
the Jewish revolt against Rome in 68 C.E. For some strange reason, the rabbis considered the Romans (and later, Christians) to
be descended from Isaac's older son Esau (a.k.a. Edom). Despite the verse from Deuteronomy cited above, the term Edomite,
in Jewish tradition, became synonymous with all oppressive rulers.

A Roman Comes to the Aid of a Jew

The day Rabbi Akiba died Rabbi Judah was born.

Judah was born at a time when the Romans had prohibited the
rite of circumcision. Rabban Simeon ben Gamaliel, his father,
said, "It is impossible for us to break Divine law and observe
the law of the Romans." So he circumcised his son.

The governor of the city learned what had happened and
summoned Rabban Simeon to appear before him.

"Why did you disobey our decree?" demanded the Roman.

"I obey the law of God," answered the rabbi.

The governor then said, "I ought to show you great honor
because you are the leader of your people. But this is the
emperor's decree, and I cannot let you go unpunished."

"Then what will you do?" asked the rabbi.

"I will send the child to the emperor, and he will do as he sees
fit."

So saying, the governor sent the baby Judah and its mother to
the Roman emperor. That whole day Judah's mother traveled
with her baby until she came to the house of a Roman lady

who was very friendly toward her. By coincidence, that lady had given birth to a baby on the very day that Judah was born.

"What are you doing here?" she asked Judah's mother.

Judah's mother then told her the whole sad story. "The Roman government prohibited the practice of circumcision. But we had our baby son circumcised, and now we have been sent to the emperor for sentencing."

The Roman lady suggested, "Look, you take my son who is not circumcised and give me your baby just for now."

Judah's mother agreed with the idea. The exchange was made and she went off with the Roman baby called Antoninus. When she arrived to the palace the emperor ordered that the baby be examined in order to establish the complaint. When it was seen that the baby was uncircumcised, the emperor flew into a rage and sent word back to the city governor saying, "My decree was against circumcision and you have been stupid enough to send an uncircumcised infant!" and Judah's mother was sent back together with the child.

Of course, on her way back she stopped off at the house of the Roman lady to return Antoninus and to receive Judah. The Roman mother said, "Since your child was saved by a miracle in which my child was involved, I hope that they will be friends for life."

> — *from Bialik and Ravnitsky, Stories of the Sages,*
> *from Sefer Ha'aggadah, selected by Chaim Pearl*

The Roman ban on circumcision began during the reign of Emperor Hadrian, who ruled from 117-138 C.E. He enacted this policy as part of a campaign against all bodily mutilation. His decision to convert Jerusalem into a Roman city and name it after himself triggered the Bar Kokhba rebellion (132-135 C.E.). Hadrian crushed it amidst massive casualties and destruction. Thereafter,

Jews were barred from Jerusalem, except once a year, on Tisha B'Av.

Hadrian's successors, a series of Emperors bearing the name "Antoninus," rescinded most of Hadrian's anti-Jewish decrees and established harmonious relations with the Jews. According to this and the following legend, one of them became close friends with Judah ha-Nasi, the Jewish sage chiefly responsible for writing down the Oral Law, *i.e.,* the Mishna, around 200 C.E.

The Rabbi and the Emperor

Antoninus confided to Rabbi Judah that he wanted his son Aswerus to succeed him and that Tiberias should be freed from taxes. "If I leave orders on one of these things it would be done" said the emperor, "but not both." When he heard this, Rabbi Judah took two men. He had one stand on the shoulders of the second, and when this was done he placed a pigeon in the hand of the man on top. Then he instructed the bottom man to tell the top man to set the bird free. Antoninus understood the advice. "He wants me to appoint Aswerus my successor and to tell him to issue the order to free Tiberias from the taxes."

Antoninus and Rabbi Judah would send each other messages in riddles. Sometimes the message would come in the form of a gift of a vegetable with a name that had to be deciphered to get the meaning of the message. Thus, one day the emperor sent the rabbi a *gargira*, which in Aramaic can mean, "My daughter committed adultery." The rabbi sent back a *kusbarta*, which in Aramaic can mean "Your daughter deserves death." The emperor replied by sending a *karta*, which can mean, "My family is dear to me." So the rabbi then sent a *chasa*, which can suggest the meaning "forgive."

Every day Antoninus sent Rabbi Judah a bag of small gold pieces. The bag was stuffed with wheat and given to a messenger with instructions to take the wheat to Rabbi Judah. The rabbi got word back to Antoninus, "I don't want your gold; I have enough of my own." The emperor replied, "Then let it be for those who follow you, and they may repay those who follow me."

Whenever they met in the emperor's palace, Antoninus served the rabbi with food and drink. Then whenever the rabbi wanted to rest, the emperor bent down saying to Judah, "Step on my back and get onto the couch." Judah refused and said he would not demean royalty in that way. On one such occasion Antoninus replied, "Would that I could be your couch on which you rest in the World to Come. Tell me rabbi, do I have a portion in the World to Come?" Judah answered, "You do." When Antoninus questioned, "But your Bible says, 'And there shall not be any remaining of the house of Esau!'" (*Ob. 1:18*). Judah replied, "But that only applies to such as behave like Esau."

When Antoninus died, Rabbi Judah lamented, "The cord is broken!"
— *from Bialik and Ravnitzky, Stories of the Sages, from Sefer Ha'Aggadah, selected by Chaim Pearl*

By assuring Antoninus that he would find a place in the next world, Rabbi Judah paid him the highest possible honor.

Since the Bible and the Talmud both contain many chauvinistic statements that the rabbis are not willing to repudiate, they have to resort to creative (some might say dishonest) interpretations to placate inquiring Gentiles. Hence, Judah, who honestly loves and respects Antoninus, dissembles in order to dismiss the plain meaning of Obadiah, a book from the Prophets. In reality, it is entirely devoted to castigating Edomites. However, there is also a passage from Talmud stating that all righteous people will have a place in Paradise.

Secular Humanistic Jews openly acknowledge this ugly side of our "sacred" texts, questioning the binding nature of such contradictory and inhumane "commandments."

A Pagan Fulfills the Fifth Commandment ... and More

They asked Rabbi Eliezer: "How far does one have to go in fulfilling the commandment about honoring one's father and one's mother?"

He replied: "Why do you ask me? You should be asking Dama ben Nethina!"

Dama ben Nethina, a pagan, was the head of the city council of Ashkelon. One day, his mother hit him with a shoe in the presence of the whole council. The shoe dropped out of her hand, but Dama picked it up and returned it to his mother, to save her the trouble of bending down.

It once happened that the jasper of the high priest's breastplate was lost. The jasper represented the tribe of Benjamin. Inquiries were made to locate someone who owned a jasper; and it was learned that Dama ben Nethina was the owner of such a precious stone.

The Sages of Israel went to Dama ben Nethina, and they reached an agreement with him that they would buy the jasper for one hundred dinars. But when Dama wanted to bring the stone, he discovered that his father was sleeping on the little chest in which the jasper was kept; and Dama refused to wake up his father on that account.

The Sages now offered him one thousand dinars; but Dama did not wake his father.

Later, when the father awoke, Dama brought the stone to the Sages. They wanted to pay him the higher price, but he said to them: "How could I sell you the honor that I owe my father?"

Instead, he sold them the jasper for the price upon which they had first agreed.

— from Petuchowski, Ed.,
Our Masters Taught: Rabbinic Stories and Sayings

Dama ben Nethina may have gone beyond the call of filial devotion in returning the shoe to his irate mother, and the Sages of Israel need not have been so impatient, but the message is clear: a pagan can also be a *mentsh*.

Dealing Honestly with All People

Once Shimon ben Shetakh bought a donkey from an Arab. When his disciples went to claim it, they found a precious jewel hanging around its neck.

They came to Shimon ben Shetakh and said, "Master, now you no longer need to work, for the Lord's blessing brings wealth."

"How is this so?" he asked them.

"We found this precious jewel on the donkey you just bought."

"Did the Arab know about this?"

"No," they answered.

"Then return it to him at once. I bought a donkey, not a jewel."

When they returned the jewel to the Arab, he exclaimed, "Blessed is the God of Shimon ben Shetakh!"

— from Frankel, The Classic Tales,
4,000 Years of Jewish Lore

Shimon ben Shetakh was a leader of the Jewish community in Palestine in the first century C.E.

It is hard to imagine why a precious jewel would be left hanging from a donkey's neck, but Shimon ben Shetakh's refusal to defraud the Arab is especially noteworthy because, according to some Talmudic authorities, defrauding non-Jews is acceptable behavior [*Baba Kamma 113 (b)*]. It is also a lesson to those elements in Israel today who have no compunction about demolishing Palestinian homes and confiscating their land.

Good Neighbors

In the year 1311, King Philip of France issued a decree ordering all Jews, under penalty of death, to be gone from his kingdom within two days. But the unfortunate Jews were unable to sell their houses, fields and household goods in such a short time. So they wandered forth without a penny and empty-handed.

One of the exiles, a wealthy dealer in precious stones and jewels who was from Paris, greatly feared that his money and jewels would be taken from him, so he confided them to the care of one of his Christian neighbors. He thought: "Some day the king's decree against the Jews may be revoked. When that will happen, I'll return and claim my treasure."

The Christian promised to guard well the money and the jewels, and so the Jew wandered forth together with all his brethren to seek an unknown refuge in the wide world.

Many years later King Philip died and his son, who inherited his throne, revoked his father's decree. He let it be known that the Jews who had been banished from the kingdom could safely return. And so the exiles returned, among them the dealer in precious gems from Paris.

The first thing the jeweler did was to call on his old neighbor to whom he had entrusted his treasure. But alas, the man was gone!

The Jew then inquired about the man among his neighbors. He learned that in recent years he had fared very badly, had lost all his possessions and was obliged to give up his fine house. Now he was living outside the city in great poverty.

Hearing this the Jew began to grieve. He was sure of one thing: if his neighbor had lost everything he must have parted company with the treasure he had entrusted to him.

Downcast, he went to look for the man outside of the city of Paris. He found him in a tiny bare hut that had neither bed nor bench. The unfortunate man was sitting on a chest, emaciated from hunger and trembling with cold. When he saw the Jew he arose and greeted him. Then he opened the chest and drew forth a bag from it. "Here is your treasure," he said. "I have guarded it well."

"How could you have done a thing like that?" cried the Jew taken aback. "You were cold and hungry and yet you did not touch these things!"

"How could I touch that which wasn't mine?" replied the Christian. "Many a time I grew weary of life and thought of death, for my suffering was too grievous to be endured. But I dared not die. Had I not faithfully promised to guard the treasure you placed in my care? I suffered and waited. It is good that you have returned now."

When the Jew heard this he was mightily moved. "How fortunate that you waited and did not take your life," he said. "Know that the hard evil days are over for you! You are my brother and half of my possessions belong to you."

So the Jew and his Christian neighbor lived side by side as of
yore, in everlasting friendship and brotherly love.
— from Ausubel, A Treasury of Jewish Folklore

This story has a happy ending, but in reality nearly all Jews were
expelled from France by the end of the fourteenth century. They
trickled back, beginning in the sixteenth century, and were finally
emancipated by the French Revolution in 1791.

The Gentiles Were Angels

The *Rebbe* of Kaliv was one the greatest of the Hungarian
*Rebbe*s. On the anniversary of his death Jews were granted the
privilege of traveling to Kaliv by train free of charge. All they
had to do was show a certificate from the city council.

It happened once that the *Rebbe* of Vizhnits sent three of his
disciples to Kaliv for the Passover holiday. When they arrived
and made their way to the *Rebbe*'s house, they found him
outside chopping wood. They greeted him in the usual fashion, and the *Rebbe* honored them with the task of carrying in
the wood. That, he said, would make them worthy of sharing
his Passover meal.

They carried in the wood and waited impatiently for the
holiday celebration to begin. Certainly the Vizhnits *Rebbe*
would not have sent them such a great distance on Passover
evening for nothing. They sat around the *seder* table expect-
antly. The *Rebbe*, smiling the same sort of enigmatic smile as
when he had bidden them carry wood, sat down with them.
Then a Gentile boy and girl arrived and helped themselves to
the Passover wine, after which all three, the *Rebbe* and the
boy and girl, danced a cheerful dance, a *freylekhs*, together.
They danced off into another room while the Vizhnits disciples looked on in dismay. What had they fallen into? "It
must be that we have stumbled into the company of Satan.
May the Merciful One help us to survive this holiday."

The *Rebbe* came back and, looking pleased, inquired, "Well, how did you like them? Not a bad couple, eh? Do you approve of their betrothal?"

When they replied that they had not come to arrange any betrothals, the *Rebbe* become disconsolate and the service proceeded in silence.

After the first days of Passover, the disciples traveled home discontentedly. It goes without saying that they were also somewhat irritated with the *Rebbe* of Vizhnits, to whom they promptly reported the disturbing Passover they had. "Ah," groaned the *Rebbe*, "fools that you are. Had you but approved of the betrothal, then the Redemption would have come. Because the two Gentiles, the boy and the girl, were actually the angels Michael and Gabriel."

                          — *from Weinreich, Ed., Yiddish Folktales*

The Gentile boy and girl were most likely called in the original Yiddish, a *sheygetz* and a *shikse*, terms that are extremely derogatory. It is that much more surprising that the disciples' refusal to approve of their engagement is blamed for preventing the coming of the Messiah.

This story is open to various interpretations. I chose to view it as one that teaches respect for Gentiles.

Chapter IX.
The Value of Education

Respect for Learning ...

There were two families that lived in Sephoris. One consisted of aristocrats, educated people who were wise in counsel. The other one consisted of common, undistinguished people.

Each day, when the two families proceeded to the house of the Nasi [the leader of the Jewish community in Roman times] to pay their respects to him, the aristocrats would enter first and the common people could go in only after the others had left.

Now it happened that these insignificant people began to apply themselves to study, and in time they became great scholars. Then they demanded that they get precedence over the aristocrats when they went to pay their respects to the Nasi.

This incident raised a great deal of discussion everywhere. When Rabbi Simeon ben Lakish was asked for an opinion, he passed the question on to Rabbi Yohanan [*i.e.,* the Nasi] who concluded: "A bastard who is a scholar is superior to a High Priest who is an ignoramus."

—from Ausubel, A Treasury of Jewish Folklore

Since the priesthood was a hereditary institution, it was bound to produce more than its share of ignoramuses. Rabbinic Judaism, in its earliest form, respected learning more than social status, although in later times, it also deferred to the rich and powerful.

It strikes me as incongruous that mainstream Jewish liturgy, to this day, includes prayers for the restoration of the Temple, which *ipso facto* means restoration of power to the priests. The Reform movement, to its credit, has eliminated all references to the Temple from its prayer books.

... and Teachers

Rabbi Judah asked Rabbi Dosa and Rabbi Ammi to go forth and inspect the cities in the land of Israel. They came to a city and said to the people, "Have the keepers of the city brought before us."

The people brought the overseers. Then they said to them: "Are these the keepers of the city?"

The people then brought forth the generals, the rich men and the strongest of the city, but the rabbis asked "Are these the keepers of the city?"

Then the people asked the rabbis: "Who then are the keepers of the city?"

The rabbis answered: "The teachers of the scriptures and the tradition, who keep watch by day and night, in accordance with these words: 'This book of law shall not depart out of thy mouth, but thou shalt meditate therein day and night.'"

— from Silverman, The Sages Speak,
Rabbinic Wisdom and Jewish Values

This story dovetails well with the bumper sticker that calls for the day when education will be fully funded and the military will have to raise money through bake sales.

Scholarship Is the Most Valuable Merchandise

A great scholar went on an ocean voyage together with a number of merchants who were conveying goods to sell in distant lands.

"What kind of merchandise do you carry?" they asked him.

"My merchandise is more valuable than yours," he answered.

But what it was he would not say.

The merchants were astonished and looked high and low in every part of the ship. But there was no sign anywhere of his goods. So they laughed at the scholar.

"He is a simpleton!" they said.

After they had sailed several days pirates attacked them and robbed the passengers of all their possessions, including the very clothes on their backs.

When the ship reached port at last, the merchants found themselves without any money or clothes. Being strangers in a foreign land, they were in a sorry plight and endured great hardships.

The scholar, on the other hand, had no sooner disembarked than he made his way to the House of Study and sat down to expound the Law. When the people saw what a learned man he was, they showed him great honor. They gave him clothing, food and lodging. When he went into the street, the dignitaries of the town escorted him with great deference.

Seeing all this, his fellow passengers, the merchants, were abashed. "Forgive us for having mocked at you." They begged him. "Help us! Intercede for us with the Elders to give us a

crust of bread, for we are hungry! Now we see that it was no idle boast when you told us that your merchandise was more valuable than ours. Learning is the best merchandise!"
— *from Ausubel, A Treasury of Jewish Folklore*

The moral of this story sounds better in the original Yiddish: *Toyre* [Torah] *iz di beste skoyre.*

But There Are Alternatives to Bible and Talmud Study

They say that when *Aher* would go into a synagogue and see children studying, he would do his best to discourage them.

"Why are these youngsters wasting their time?" he would ask. "This one can become a builder, the other one a carpenter and the third can become a tailor!" The youngsters were impressionable and were influenced to leave the school.

Aher was always singing Greek songs and carrying heretical books.
— *adapted from Bialik and Ravnitsky, Stories of the Sages, from Sefer Ha'aggadah, selected by Chaim Pearl*

Aher, which means "the other," was the name the rabbis used for Elisha ben Abuyah, a famed second century C.E. Talmudic sage, after he became an apostate and rejected Jewish religious doctrine. (See also "Rabbi Meir Learns from a Heretic," in Chapter III.) Education lacking in humanistic values is not a virtue, as can readily be seen in certain *yeshivot* here and in Israel that shun secular subjects, fail to teach practical skills and promote religious fanaticism.

How to Teach an Unwilling Student

A long time ago there lived a King and Queen and their son the Prince. They considered this prince to be their jewel, their greatest treasure, the apple of their eye. The King made certain that the Prince had the most learned teachers and the wisest soothsayers to instruct him in all that a prince would need to know in order to be a great king when the time came for him to rule the kingdom.

One day, a strange illness overcame the Prince, and he began to act like a rooster. He took off his clothes and roamed all around the palace, flapping his arms like a rooster and crowing loud and long. He also stopped speaking the language of the King and Queen. He ate only corn from the floor, like a rooster, and refused to sit at the table with others, eating only under the table alone.

The King and Queen became very upset and called for the best doctors in the kingdom to treat the Prince, in hopes of curing him of the illness. But nothing that the doctors and the soothsayers and the other healers tried seemed to make any difference, and the Rooster Prince continued happily crowing and flapping his arms, and hopping around in the palace, wherever he wanted to go.

One day, a wise old man came to the palace. "Your Majesty, I would like to try to cure the Prince," he said to the King.

"Where are your medicines?" asked the surprised King, because all the doctors carried at least one bag filled with bottles of potions and oils.

"I have my own ways, Your Majesty," answered the wise man. "Allow me seven days alone with the Prince."

The King reluctantly agreed, since there was no other hope. The wise man was brought to the Prince. The first thing he did was to take off all his clothes, jump under the table and sit opposite the Rooster Prince.

The Prince stared at the stranger for a very long time. "Who are you, and what are you doing here?" crowed the Rooster Prince curiously.

"I am a rooster, Can't you see that?" answered the wise man matter-of-factly but patiently.

"Oh, I am a rooster, too. Welcome!" replied the Prince, happy to have found a friend.

Time passed with the two companions crowing and flapping their arms.

One day, the stranger got out from under the table and began to walk around, a little straighter each day. The Rooster Prince had grown so fond of this friend that he began to follow him wherever he went. And the two roosters hopped around the palace together.

On another day, the wise man put on a shirt and a pair of trousers. "What are you wearing, my friend?" asked the Rooster Prince. "Roosters don't wear clothes!"

"You're right, dear Prince, but I was a bit chilled. However, I assure you, you can still be a good rooster even with clothes on. Try it," challenged the wise man.

The Rooster Prince put some clothes on, too, and continued crowing and flapping his arms.

The next day, the wise man sat at the table and ate some corn from a golden platter. The Rooster Prince sat next to his friend. The wise man signaled to the servants and soon the table was set with silverware, goblets, and golden plates. Slowly, the wise man began to eat all the delicious foods — in a proper manner — and the Prince began to imitate him. Soon a whole meal was eaten, and the Rooster Prince crowed most happily.

The following night, the wise man began to sleep on a bed. He again assured the Prince. "Don't worry, my Prince, you can be a good rooster just the same, even sleeping on a bed." And so the Rooster Prince resumed sleeping on his royal bed and no longer slept under the table.

Soon after, the wise man began to discuss the philosophy of life with the Prince. "Wait a minute, roosters don't have to think, and they certainly don't debate the merits of a way of life," declared the Prince. "Roosters just exist, being fed and cared for without any worries."

"You may be right," answered his wise old friend, "but on the other hand, it doesn't mean you can't be a good rooster if you do engage in discussion. After all, you will know that you are a rooster, just the same."

The Prince thought this over and began to discuss philosophical ideas with the wise man.

On the seventh day, the wise man bid farewell to the Prince. As he was about to leave, he said, "My friend, remember, roosters are fair game for the hunter. So always try to pretend you are a human prince. Act wisely and help others. Farewell!"

From that day on, the Prince walked, ate and talked like the prince he was. And when, in time, he became a great King ruling over that entire kingdom, no one besides himself knew that he was still a rooster.
> — *from Jewish Stories One Generation Tells Another,*
> *retold by Peninnah Schram*

This story provides amazing insights into human psychology. It gives new meaning to the expression about getting down to another person's level.

Chapter X.
Parents & Children

Honor Thy Father and Thy Mother

In a certain city lived a rich man who had three sons. Two had left home to seek their fortunes in a distant town. One prospered but the other became poverty-stricken. Many years passed since they had left home, but one day their father wrote them a letter inviting them to attend the wedding of their youngest brother.

The letter was addressed to the son who had prospered. It read, in part, "Return home, my son, and be sure to bring with you your poor brother so that we may all rejoice together. I promise to pay all the traveling expenses that you may incur in fulfilling the Commandment, 'Honor thy father and thy mother.'"

Immediately after reading the letter the wealthy son paid a visit to all the dry goods shops where he bought the most expensive materials for himself, his wife and children. Then he began feverish preparations for the wedding.

When they were all ready to start and the horses were harnessed for the journey, the wealthy son suddenly recalled that he had forgotten to extend his father's invitation to his poor brother. So he called out to his servants, "Make haste and call my brother! Bring him here as quickly as possible and tell him that it's important!"

His servants did as he bid them and brought back his poor
brother who, all out of breath, said, "I'm greatly surprised,
brother, that you've called me. I can't understand why you
should suddenly develop an interest in me after neglecting me
for all these years."

"Ask no questions!" his rich brother replied. "Get into the
carriage and come with me!"

And so the poor brother climbed into the carriage and away
they whirled.

Upon their arrival their father and all the relatives came out to
welcome them with great joy. First to alight from the carriage
was the wealthy son, dressed up like a lord. Then followed his
wife and children, dazzling in their finery. Passersby inquired
with curiosity, "Who is this prince?"

And the relatives answered, "Why don't you know? This is
the son of the town's richest man, and he himself is very rich
too."

Then, with great embarrassment, the poor brother slunk out of
the carriage. His clothes were threadbare and there were
patches on his shoes.

"And who is this one?" asked the passersby in astonishment.

"Oh, he?" evasively replied the relatives, somewhat ashamed.
"He is from the same town."

"Maybe he's his brother or some other relative?" asked the
passerby, slyly.

The relatives did not answer.

The rich son and his family stayed two weeks in the house of his father. Then he said, "Dear father, as you see I have obeyed you in everything you've asked of me. I came to rejoice with you, but you know that I'm a merchant and my time is valuable, so as much as I regret it, I must prepare for the journey home."

"Do what is best for you, my son," his father answered.

When the son was ready to depart he was filled with chagrin, for his father, who had promised to pay him all his expenses and give him a fine gift besides, did not even mention a word about it. So he handed him an itemized bill: so much and so much for his clothes, his wife's, his children's, so much and so much for what it cost him in the inns at which he stopped on the way, as well as for several other items.

"How nice!" said his father. "I am happy, my son, to see that you can afford such fine expensive clothes! May you, your wife and children wear them in good health."

"It isn't that, father," replied his son in embarrassment. "Let me remind you of your promise that you'd repay me for all my expenses for the wedding."

The father regarded his son in astonishment. "I never made any such promise!" he insisted.

Without a word, the son handed his father the letter of invitation he had sent him, saying, "There it is, in your own handwriting!"

His father then took the letter from him and read what he had written aloud, pronouncing each word very carefully: "I promise to pay all the traveling expenses that you may incur in fulfilling the Commandment, 'Honor thy father and thy mother.'"

"There, you see!" cried his son triumphantly.

"Now, just let us understand what it is I wrote to you," said his father. Had you really wished to honor me you would have taken pity upon your poor brother and not brought him here dressed in tatters. You would have known that the way to honor me was to clothe him decently. So you see, therefore, that the expenses you incurred for the wedding were only for your honor. And these, my son, I did not promise to pay for."
— from Ausubel, A Treasury of Jewish Folklore

To shame someone is considered a grave sin in Jewish law. To shame a close relative can only be worse. Why does the father choose to teach this lesson by refusing to pay his son's expenses? Perhaps he realizes that money is the only thing his son understands.

A Parents' Responsibility

Rabbi Huna, citing Rabbi Yochanan, told the parable of a man who opened a perfume shop for his son on a street inhabited by prostitutes. The prostitutes plied their trade, the perfume store owners plied theirs, and the boy, like any young man, indulged his natural inclination, and fell into depraved ways. When the father came and caught him with a prostitute, he began to shout, "I'll kill you!" But the father's friend was there and said: "You yourself ruined your son, and now you are yelling at him! You ignored all other occupations and taught him to be a perfumer; you ignored all other streets and deliberately opened a shop for him in the street of prostitutes!" (*Midrash, Exodus Rabbah 43:7*).
— from Telushkin, Jewish Wisdom

In the age-old debate over the source of human frailties, this story comes down squarely on the side of "nurture" rather than "nature." Except in cases of physiological disorder, this is the only explanation of human behavior that is consistent with a humanistic world view. We are more than the sum of our genes.

Respect for the Elderly
(or Teach Your Children Well)

There once was a rich man who took no care of his father. One winter day, when the man's small son found his grandfather trembling with cold, he went and told him about it. "Son," said the rich man, "take that torn overcoat lying in the corner and give it to the old fellow to cover his hide with."

The boy took the overcoat out to the yard, spread it on the ground, and before the eyes of the entire family, began cutting it in half with scissors.

"What are you doing?" asked the rich man.

"I'm giving half the overcoat to your father and saving the other half for you when you grow old," replied the boy.
— *from Jewish Folktales, selected and retold by Pinhas Sadeh*

⌘ ⌘ ⌘

Once an old man lived in his only son's house. Life was cheerful for him, since he had his own room and a place for his books and for studying. When it came time for meals, the whole family gathered at the big round dining table to eat together. The son and the wife treated him well. Soon there was a grandchild, and the old man took great pleasure in watching his grandson grow. He loved to take the child on his lap and tell him stories.

As the years went by, the old man's hands began to shake, at first only a little. Sometimes he would spill his tea because of his trembling hands, or he would drop a plate. And little by little his son became more and more impatient with him.

One day as the whole family was sitting at the dinner table, the old man accidentally hit his plate with the soup spoon and the plate broke, spilling the soup on the tablecloth and onto his lap. His son threw down his spoon and jumped up angrily, shouting, "If you can't eat like a *mentsh*, eat alone. I'm tired of your spilling food on our good tablecloths and breaking our good dishes!"

The next day, the son brought home a wooden plate. He then set a table in the old man's bedroom, using an old sheet as a tablecloth, and served him his food on the wooden plate.

The old man said nothing and ate his meals alone day after day. But to be separated from his family in this way hurt him very much.

One day, when the son came home from work, he noticed his young child working at a task in the corner. "Well, my big son, what keeps you so busy today?" he asked.

"I'm making a plate, carving it from wood all by myself," answered the little boy.

His father was surprised. "A plate of wood? What will you use that for? We have beautiful dishes."

And the little boy answered, "I know, Father. But I'm making this plate for you, when you grow old like Grandfather. And when your hands begin to shake, why then I'll have this wooden plate ready to give you in your little room."

When the father heard this, he ran to his father and fell to his knees. "Forgive me, my father. Forgive me for not showing you the respect and honor due you." And he wept.

Yes, the father forgave his son. And that evening the family sat together at the big round table.

As for the old man, he sat at the place of honor.
— *from Jewish Stories One Generation Tells Another,*
retold by Peninnah Schram

These stories reflect the basic truth that children learn more from their parent's deeds than from their words. They also raise difficult issues facing many families who must confront the dilemma of how to best care for aging parents.

Chapter XI.
Friendship

Rabbi Alexandri said: Two donkey drivers who hated each
other were waiting on a road when the donkey of one lay
down under its burden. His companion saw it, and at first he
passed on. But then he reflected: Is it not written in the Torah,
"If you see your enemy's donkey lying down under its burden
and are reluctant to help him raise it, you must help him
nevertheless" (*Exod. 23:4, Deut. 22:4*). So then he returned,
lent a hand and helped his enemy: "Release a bit here, pull up
over there, unload over here." Thus peace came about between them, so that the driver of the overloaded donkey said,
"Did I not assume that he hated me? But look how compassionate he has been." By and by, the two entered an inn, ate
and drank together and became fast friends [*Tanhuma,
Mishpatim #1 (Midrash atttributed to Tanhuma bar Abba, a
late third century rabbi)*].

— *from Telushkin, Jewish Wisdom*

It is all too easy to look the other way when someone we dislike is
in trouble. Some may even derive satisfaction from another's misfortune. This is the meaning of the German term *Schadenfreude*.
Judaism does not require someone to love his or her enemy, but
helping an enemy in need is our ethical obligation.

⌘⌘⌘

Moses Leib, the Hasidic rabbi of Sassov, declared to his
disciples: "I learned how we must truly love our neighbor

from the conversation between two villagers, which I overheard. The first said: 'Tell me, friend Ivan, do you love me?'
The second: 'I love you deeply.' The first: 'Do you know, my
friend, what gives me pain?' The second: 'How can I know
what gives you pain?' The first: 'If you do not know what
gives me pain, how can you say that you truly love me?'
Understand then, my sons, to love, to truly love, means to
know what brings pain to your fellow human being."
— *from Silverman, The Sages Speak:*
Rabbinic Wisdom and Jewish Values

An important sub-text of this story is that the villagers are obviously Christian peasants, who were commonly stereotyped as
ignorant drunkards.

⌘⌘⌘

Once a disciple of Rabbi Akiba became ill and no one visited
him. Rabbi Akiba, however, entered the sick man's room,
arranged that it be swept and cleared, placed the pillow in
order and the like. All this assisted the recovery of the disciple. He exclaimed, "O master, thou hast revived me." When
Rabbi Akiba departed, he said: "Whoever neglects to visit a
friendless, sick person is as if he shed blood."
— *from Browne, Ed., The Wisdom of Israel*

Rabbi Akiba ben Joseph (50-135 C.E.) was one of the architects
of the Talmud and a highly honored sage. In his old age, he supported the Bar Kokhba revolt, even going so far as proclaiming
him the messiah. Akiba died a martyr's death at the hands of the
Romans.

Another legend, not included here, extols him for refusing to interrupt his teaching of Torah to attend to his dying son. *Feh*!

⌘⌘⌘

Once when Honi was out walking, he came upon a man planting a carob tree.

"How long will it be before this tree bears fruit?" Honi asked.

"Seventy years," the man replied.

"How do you know you'll be alive in seventy years?"

"Just as I found carob trees when I came into the world," answered the man, "so I am now planting carob trees for my grandchildren to enjoy."

Then Honi lay down and fell asleep. While he slept, a rock enveloped him so that he slept undetected for seventy years. When he awoke, he saw a man gathering carobs under a nearby tree.

"Did you plant this tree?" Honi asked him.

"No, my grandfather did," answered the man.

"Then I have been sleeping for seventy years!" cried Honi.

Then he went to his house. "Does Honi the Circle-Maker still live here?" he asked.

"No," they told him. "he died long ago, but his grandson lives here."

"I am Honi," he said. But they didn't believe him.

He went to the House of Study and sat in the back of the room. The rabbis were discussing the Law, and they said, "This teaching is as clear to us as it was in the days of Honi the Circle-Maker. They say he used to come here and answer all the rabbis' questions."

Honi stood up and declared, "I am Honi!"

But they didn't believe him, either. He prayed for mercy, and he soon died.

Later Rava taught, "That is why people say 'Either give me fellowship, or give me death.'"

— adapted from Frankel,
The Classic Tales, 4000 Years of Jewish Lore

This is a famous story about a Jewish Rip Van Winkle. Although he lives to see his grandchild enjoy the fruits of his labor, even that degree of *nakhes* cannot compensate for his loneliness. A Yiddish expression conveys the same message: *Eyner iz keyner* (one, alone, is no one).

Chapter XII.
The Sanctity
of
Human Life

Unlike other parts of the Creation, man was created alone. This teaches us that whoever kills one man is as if he destroyed all mankind. Conversely, whoever saves one life is as though he had saved the whole world.

The creation of a single man was also for the sake of peace, so that no man will ever be able to say to another "My ancestor was greater than yours."

The individuality of each human being is also implied here. Because while a man who mints many coins from one mold will make each the same, God, who made every human being after the pattern of the first *Adam*, made every man different. Hence each individual is entitled to claim "The world was created for my sake."

Our sages taught: why was man created alone? In order to prevent all kinds of theories from both the righteous and wicked to explain or excuse their behavior. If more than one man had been created, then the righteous might have thought, "we are descendants of the good ancestor" and the wicked would have excused themselves by saying "We are the children of the bad ancestor."

— from Bialik and Ravnitsky,
Sefer Ha-Aggadah, The Book of Jewish Folklore and Legend,
selected by Chaim Pearl

Despite these admirable sentiments, the Bible explicitly distinguishes between "good ancestors" and "bad ancestors." The descendants of Shem are deemed superior to the descendants of Ham (Shem and Ham being two of Noah's sons); the descendants of Isaac superior to the descendants of Ishmael (Isaac and Ishmael being Abraham's sons); and the descendants of Jacob superior to the descendants of Esau (Jacob and Esau being Isaac's sons).

God, having declared the Hebrews his "Chosen People," authorized them to exterminate the Canaanites and six other nations who occupied the "Promised Land" before them. These peoples didn't even deserve to have ancestors. Centuries later, Ezra, the editor of the Torah, declared the Samaritans, a closely related people, to be pariahs and forced Jewish men to divorce their non-Jewish wives.

As Spinoza observed, there has always been an inherent conflict between the concept of a universal ethical God and the doctrine of the Chosen People. The stories in this chapter (and in Chapter VII, "Jewish-Gentile Relations") emphasize the universalist side of Jewish tradition, embraced by Secular Humanistic Jews.

⌘⌘⌘

In response to Cain's inquiry, "Am I my brother's
keeper?" God answered: "The voice of thy brother's
blood crieth unto Me from the ground" (Genesis 4:10).

Rabbi Simeon ben Yohai taught: This may be compared to the case of men on a ship, one of whom took a borer and began boring beneath his own place. His fellow travelers said to him: "What are you doing?" Said he to them: "What does that matter to you? Am I not boring under my own place?" Said they: "Because the water will come up and flood the ship for us all. What we do influences the security of our fellow men. Man is ever responsible for his brother's welfare."

— from Silverman, The Sages Speak: Rabbinic Wisdom and Jewish Values

⌘⌘⌘

Said Rabbi Bunam: No Jew, however learned and pious, may consider himself an iota better than a fellow Jew, however ignorant or irreligious the latter may be. This is confirmed in the law that if a learned and pious Jew were commanded to slay the ignorant and impious one, or be himself slain, he must accept death rather than kill another. No one can tell whose blood is redder and whose life is more important in the eyes of God. If a man in this crucial moment has no right to deem himself superior to another, what right can he possibly have to do so on less critical occasions?

— from Newman and Spitz, The Hasidic Anthology

⌘⌘⌘

Simchah Bunam (1765-1827) was a Hasidic rabbi from Poland. It is unclear whether he would have extended this principle to non-Jews. Not all rabbis did.

⌘⌘⌘

On Yom Kippur, the Berditchever *Rebbe* was summoned to Heaven to defend the case of a criminal. After convincing God to forgive the man, he took it upon himself to insist that God forgive the entire world. He argued so passionately that God was about to grant his appeal and send the Messiah to end the world's misery and suffering.

Just at that moment, the *Rebbe* realized that, back on earth, Yom Kippur was drawing to an end and that his congregation was waiting for him to lead the final prayer so they would be free to break their fasts. Suddenly the *Rebbe* saw Hirsch, a poor old Jew, falling to the floor. Now Hirsh was often hungry on normal days and the effects of a total day's fast were taking a severe toll. The *Rebbe* believed that unless he concluded the service immediately, Hirsch would die on the spot. So he said to God: "Perhaps I am about to make the mistake of my life because in another minute I think I can convince you to send the Messiah, but Hirsch's life is at stake. But where is it written that I have the right to sacrifice Hirsch's life for the sake all humanity?"

> — *retold from Joshua Rubenstein,*
> *Tangled Loyalties, The Life and Times of Ilya Ehrenburg,*
> *in which he relates a passage from Ehrenburg's,*
> *The Story of Lasik Roitchwantz*

The sacrifice of human life to a "higher cause" can be a noble deed when people make this choice for themselves. However, when any arbitrary authority decides that other people must sacrifice their lives, we must make the preservation of human life our top priority. From a secular humanistic perspective, the ends, no matter how worthy, definitely do *not* justify the means.

Ehrenburg (1891-1967), a prominent Soviet journalist and writer, failed to live up to this principle by supporting Stalin's dictatorship, although he distinguished himself as a forceful advocate of greater freedom of expression during the post-Stalin era. The novel where this story can be found was written in the 1920s, before he threw in his lot with Stalinism. I cannot find it in any other source, so I assume Ehrenburg learned it directly from a Hasidic story teller.

Chapter XIII.
The Evil of Slander

One day a young woman came to the rabbi of her community and confessed that she had been in the habit of telling falsehoods and spreading lies about her neighbors. She asked his help to enable her to make amends.

"Pluck a chicken," he told her, "and scatter the feathers all the way from your home to mine. Gather them up again and bring them to me and I will then give you my answer."

Eagerly she promised to do this and left.

The following day she returned and said: "Rabbi, I did as you instructed me — plucked the chicken and scattered its feathers — but I regret that I couldn't bring them here, because when I tried to pick them up I discovered the wind had blown them in all directions."

"Yes, my child," replied the rabbi sadly, "lies are like feathers; once scattered, it is impossible to retrieve them. Nor can the damage they have done ever be recalled or completely amended. Henceforth, resolve to speak the truth only."
> — *from Silverman, The Sages Speak:*
> *Rabbinic Wisdom and Jewish Values*

⌘ ⌘ ⌘

One day the members of the animal kingdom will assemble to reproach the serpent: "If the lion rends his prey, it is because he is hungry. If the wolf devours his victim, it is because he must eat. But you, O serpent! What profit do you get from biting others?"

And the serpent, being very clever, will reply: "Am I worse than the slanderer?"
— *from Nathan Ausubel, The Book of Jewish Knowledge*

... and a Humane Cure

The story is told that Samuel Ha-Nagid, an eleventh century Spanish-Jewish poet who was prime minister to the king of Granada, was once insulted by an enemy in the presence of the king. The king was so angered that he ordered his prime minister to punish the offender by cutting out his tongue. Contrary to the king's mandate, Samuel treated his enemy with the utmost kindness. When the king learned that his order had not been carried out, he was greatly astonished. Samuel was ready with a pleasant answer. He said, "I have carried out your order, Your Majesty. I have cut out his evil tongue and have given him instead a kindly tongue."
— *from Bernard S. Raskas, Heart of Wisdom*

Samuel Ha-Nagid or Samuel Ibn Nagrela (993-1056) was the vizier (chief advisor) to the king of Granada and, as a general, led its armies into battle. His title, *Nagid* indicates that he was also the recognized leader of the kingdom's Jewish community. In this capacity, he made major efforts to improve the legal status of his fellow Jews.

Samuel Ha-Nagid must have been held in high esteem for this story to be written about him. How many people would evade the orders of a supreme authority figure for the sake of saving an offensive person from punishment? It reflects a perspective that values reconciliation over revenge.

Chapter XIV.
Some Humanistic
Principles to Live By
from *Pirke Avot*

Shemaya [the head of the Sanhedrin, the Jewish court and legislature, during the second half of the first century B.C.E.] said: Love work, hate domineering over others and do not seek the intimacy of public officials.

There are four types of character among people. He who says: "What is mine is mine and what is yours is yours" is a medium type. ... He who says: "What is mine is yours and what is yours is mine" is an ignoramus. He who says: "What is mine is yours and what is yours is yours" is a saintly man. He who says: "What is yours is mine and what is mine is mine" is a wicked man.

Hillel said: Do not separate yourself from the community, and do not be sure of yourself until the day you die; do not judge your fellow-man until you have been put in his position; do not make pronouncements that cannot be understood at once in the confident thought that they will be understood later on; and do not say that you will study when you will have leisure, for you may never attain to leisure.

He used to say: An uncultured man cannot really fear sin; an
ignorant man cannot be truly pious; a bashful man cannot
learn and an impatient man cannot teach; he who engages in
much commerce does not necessarily become wise; and in a
place where there are no men [decent people], strive to be a
man [a decent person].

Rabbi Hanina ben Dosa said: He whose deeds exceed his
wisdom, his wisdom will endure; he whose wisdom exceeds
his deeds, his wisdom will not endure.

And Finally ...

It is not your obligation to complete the task [of perfecting the
world], but neither are you free to desist [from doing your
part].

— Rabbi Tarfon

Chapter XV.
Why Remain Jewish?

As everyone knows, Rabbi Jonathan was constantly engaged in debate with the greatest people in the nation over matters of faith.

The rabbi had a keen intelligence and he was a God-fearing man, as everyone knew. A story is told about a minister who, meaning to test Rabbi Jonathan's intelligence, sent a messenger inviting him for a visit. However, the minister instructed his servants not to tell the rabbi where in the palace he was to be found.

Reb Jonathan came to the palace and asked to be shown to the minister's room. One guard replied that he was in such-and such a room; another guard gave the rabbi quite different directions. And so with all the guards: they gave him contradictory answers and directions. Finally the rabbi paused and, thinking the matter over, decided that the minister must be in a particular room. He went to it and, indeed, there was the minister.

When the rabbi presented himself, the minister was amazed. "Ha! How did you know I would be in this room? Who told you?"

"How could anyone have told me, since all your Swiss guards gave me contradictory directions? Now we Jews have a

saying, 'Follow the majority.' And that's what I did. I thought
through everything they told me and counted up the replies. It
was clear that this was the room, so I went to it."

"In that case," said the minister, "why is it that you Jews don't
follow the majority in today's world? Why do you insist on
being a minority among the nations?"

The rabbi thought for a while, then he said, "In the palace, I
followed the majority because I knew that you were here.
What was in doubt was which room you were in. But we Jews
have no doubts about where we are in the world. And that is
why we don't accept conversion and remain a distinct
people."

— from Weinreich, Ed., Yiddish Folktales

The Rabbi Jonathan referred to in this story is supposed to be
Jonathan Eybeschutz (1690-1764), who lived in Prague, Metz
(France) and Altona (a German-speaking city in Denmark).

Although many of us cannot be as certain as Rabbi Eybeschutz
about our place in the world and can perhaps think of better reasons to remain Jewish, this story illustrates two important principles: the necessity to respect majority opinion and the equally
compelling necessity to dissent if following the majority would cause
us to lose our identity as Jews and violate our most cherished
beliefs.

Acknowledgments

The following selections from *A Treasury of Jewish Folklore* by Nathan Ausubel (©1948, 1976, Crown Publishers) are reprinted by permission of Crown Publishers, a division of Random House, Inc:

A Tailor's Prayer, Fair Solution, The Rabbi Who Wished to Abolish Death, He Should Have Taken More Time, The Right Kind of Judge, Nebich!, No Target, The Lord Helpeth Man and Beast, His Brother's Keeper, The Veneer of Silver, The Piety of the Heart, Qualifications For Paradise, The Saint and the Sinner, Caught in His Own Trap, Equal Justice, True Piety, The Father of the Poor (last story only), The Limits of Piety, The Golden Ladder of Charity, The Good Job, Adding Insult to Injury, The Poor Man's Miracle, Consolation to the Pious, The Gulden Test, Hershl's Conflict, Absent- Minded, A Fool Asks Too Many Questions, From Bad to Worse, The Rabbi and the Rebbetzin, God Protects the Heathen, The Faithful Neighbor, Learning Knows No Class, The Most Valuable Merchandise, By Loving Man You Honor God (excluding last paragraph), A Worthy Companion, Adding Insult to Injury

The following selections from *Yiddish Folktales* by Beatrice Weinreich Silverman (©1988, by YIVO Institute for Jewish Research) are reprinted by permission of Pantheon Books, a division of Random House, Inc.:

The Sacrifice of Isaac and the Caretaker of Brisk, Holding On to One-Quarter of My World, The Happy Pair and the Baal Shem Tov, Skotsl Kumt: Skotl's Here, The Missed Moment of Redemption, Rabbi Jonathan and the Minister: A Disputation

(©1988 by Dvir Publishing House) are used by permission of Dvir
Publishing House:
> Excerpts from The Great Lamentation, The Golden Calf,
> Sodom and Gomorrah, The Roman Attack and Man

The following selections from *Sefer Ha' Aggadah, Stories of the
Sages* by Hayyim Bialik and Yehoshua Ravnitsky, selected, trans-
lated and annotated by Chaim Pearl (©1991 by Dvir Publishing
House) are used by permission of Dvir Publishing House:
> Untitled stories, pp.60-61, 108, 116, 116-117, 121-122, 127,
> 138-140, 147-148, 160-162, excerpts from The Schools of
> Shammai and Hillel

The following selections from *The Classic Tales, 4000 Thousand
Years of Jewish Lore* by Ellen Frankel (©1989 by Jason Aronson
Inc.) are reprinted by permission of the publisher, Jason Aronson,
Inc, Northvale, NJ:
> The Wooden Sword, Rashi's Companion, The Great Power of
> Psalms, Let Them Eat Stones, Lilith, Elijah and the Three
> Wishes, Soft Like a Reed — Not Hard Like a Cedar, The
> Hidden Jewel of Shimon ben Shetakh, excerpts from Honi and
> the Carob Tree and The Ugly Wise Girl

The following selections from *The Sages Speak: Rabinical Wisdom
and Jewish Values* by William Silverman (©1995 by Jason
Aronson Inc.) are reprinted by permission of the publisher, Jason
Aronson, Inc., Northvale, NJ:
> Untitled selections pp.29-30, 31-32, 83-84, 104-105, 108-109,
> 121,144, 198-199, 224

The following selections from *Jewish Stories One Generation Tells
Another* by Peninnah Schram (©1989 by Jason Aronson, Inc.) are
reprinted by permission of the publisher, Jason Aronson, Inc.,
Northvale, NJ:
> The Rooster Who Would be King, Three Generations

The following selection from *Chosen Tales: Stories Told by Jewish Storytellers* by Peninnah Scham (©1995 by Jason Aronson, Inc.) is reprinted by permission of the publisher, Jason Aronson, Inc., Northvale, NJ:
> pp. 282-283, about Joha

The following selection from *The Legends of the Rabbis, Vol. I, Jewish Legends of the Second Commonwealth* by Judah Nadich (©1994 by Jason Aronson, Inc.) is reprinted by permission of the publisher, Jason Aronson, Inc., Northvale, NJ:
> The Destruction of Jerusalem and the Temple

The following selections from *A Rabbinic Anthology* by C.G. Montefiore and H. Loewe (©1960 by The Jewish Publication Society) are used by permission of The Jewish Publication Society:
> Numbered selections 665, 1157

The following selections from *Legends of the Bible* by Louis Ginsberg, Jewish Publication Society (©1956) are used by permission of The Jewish Publication Society:
> Excerpts from untitled stories on p.72 and p.599-600, excerpts from The Rebellion of Korah and Korah Abuses Moses and the Torah

The following selection from *Ma'aseh Book: Book of Jewish Tales and Legends, Vol. One* (©1934) is used by permission of The Jewish Publication Society:
> The Humility of Hillel

The following selections from *The Talmudic Anthology: Tales and Teachings of the Rabbis* by Louis I. Newman and Samuel Spitz, published by Behrman House, Inc., 235 Watchung Ave. W. Orange, NJ 07054 (©1945) are used with permission of Behrman House Inc.:
> The Diligent and the Lazy, untitled selections on pp. 176, 230, 441, 540

The following selections from *Jewish Wisdom* by Joseph Telushkin (©1994, William Morrow and Company, Inc.) are used by permission of HarperCollins, Inc.:
Untitled selections on pp. 31-32, 116, 158, 191-192, 196, 286-287, 349, The Dangers of Asceticism

The following selections from *Our Masters Taught: Rabbinic Stories and Sayings* by Jakob J. Petuchowski, Crossroads Publishing Company (©1982) are used by permission of Elizabeth Petuchowski:
Honoring Father and Mother, Words of the Living God, He Threw Away The Peel

The following selections from *Mimekor Yisrael, Selected Classical Jewish Folktales* by Micha Joseph Bin Gurion (©1990 by Indiana University Press) are used by permission of Indiana University Press:
The Parable of the Precious Stones, The Golem: The Fashioning of the Golem, The Golem: The Death of the Golem

The following selections from *Jewish Folktales* by Pincus Sadeh, translated by Hillel Halkin (©1989 by Doubleday, a division of Bantam Doubleday Dell Publishing Group, Inc.) are used by permission of Doubleday, a division of Random House, Inc.:
The Boy Who Cut an Overcoat in Half, The Man Who Agreed to Be Moses, The Debate Between the Priest and the Town Fool, excerpts from King Solomon and Queen Kehira

The following selection from the *Encyclopedia of Jewish Humor* by Henry D. Spalding (©1969 by Jonathan David Publishers, Inc.) is used by permission of Jonathan David Publishers, Inc.:
The first untitled selection on p.11, excluding the first paragraph

The following selection from *The Folklore of the Jews* by Angelo S. Rappoport (©1937 by Soncino Press) London is used by permission of The Soncino Press, Ltd.:
The Flourishing Staff, pp. 206-7

Bibliography

Arnold, Abraham J., *Judaism: Myth, Legend, History and Custom, from the Religious to the Secular* (Quebec, Canada: Robert Davies Publishing, 1995).

Ausubel, Nathan, *A Treasury of Jewish Folklore* (New York: Crown Publishers, 1948).

Ausubel, Nathan, *The Book of Jewish Knowledge* (New York: Crown Publishers, 1964).

Bialik, Hayyim and Ravnitzky, Yehoshua, *Sefer Ha'Aggadah, The Book of Jewish Folklore and Legend (Vol. I)*, and *Stories of the Sages (Vol. II)*, selected, translated and annotated by Chaim Pearl (Tel Aviv, Israel: Dvir Publishing House, 1988, 1991).

Bin Gurion, Micha Joseph, *Mimekor Yisrael, Selected Classical Jewish Folktales* (Bloomington, Indiana: Indiana University Press, 1990).

Browne, Lewis, *The Wisdom of Israel: an Anthology* (New York: The Modern Library, 1945).

Buber, Martin, *Tales of the Hasidim, The Early Masters* (New York: Schocken Books, 1947).

Buber, Martin, *Tales of the Hasidim, The Later Masters* (New York: Schocken Books, 1948).

Dawidowicz, Lucy, *The Golden Tradition: Jewish Life and Thought in Eastern Europe* (New York: Schocken Books, 1967).

Frankel, Ellen, *The Classic Tales, 4000 Years of Jewish Lore* (Northvale, N.J.: Jason Aronson, 1989).

Gaster, Moses, *Ma'aseh Book, Vol. I* (Philadelphia: Jewish Publication Society, 1934).

Ginzberg, Louis, *Legends of the Bible* (Philadephia: Jewish Publication Society, 1956).

Glatzer, Nahum N., *Hammer on the Rock, A Short Midrash Reader* (New York: Schocken Books, 1948).

Goodman, Saul, *The Faith of Secular Jews* (New York: KTAV Publishing House, Inc., 1976).

Goodspeed, Edgar G., *The Apochrypha, an American Translation* (New York: Modern Library, 1959).

Holtz, Barry, *Finding Our Way: Jewish Texts and the Lives We Live Today* (New York: Schocken Books, 1990).

Howe, Irving and Greenberg, Eliezer, *A Treasury of Yiddish Stories* (New York: Schocken Books, 1973).

Laytner, Anson, *Arguing With God — A Jewish Tradition* (Northvale, N.J.: Jason Aronson, Inc., 1990).

Montefiore, C.G. and Loewe, H., *A Rabbinic Anthology* (Philadelphia: Jewish Publication Society, 1960).

Nadich, Judah, *The Legends of the Rabbis, Vol. I, Jewish Legends of the Second Commonwealth* (Northvale, N.J.: Jason Aronson, Inc., 1994).

Nahmad, H. M., *A Portion of Paradise and Other Jewish Folktales* (Washington, D.C.: B'nai B'rith Commission on Adult Jewish Education, 1970).

Newman, Louis I., and Spitz, Samuel, *The Talmudic Anthology: Tales and Teachings of the Rabbis* (New York: Behrman House, Inc., 1945).

Patai, Raphael, *Gates to the Old City: A Book of Jewish Legends* (Northvale, N.J.: Jason Aronson, Inc., 1988).

Petuchowski, Jakob J., *Our Masters Taught: Rabbinic Stories and Sayings* (New York: Crossroad Publishing, 1982).

Rappoport, Angelo S., *The Folklore of the Jews* (New York: Soncino Press, 1937).

Raskas, Bernard, *The Heart of Wisdom: A Thought for Each Day of the Jewish Year* (New York: Burning Bush Press, 1962).

Rosenfeld, Max, *Festivals, Folklore and Philosophy: A Secularist Revisits Jewish Tradition* (Philadelphia: Sholem Aleichem Club of Philadelphia, 1997).

Sadeh, Pinkus, *Jewish Folktales* (New York: Doubleday, 1989).

Schram, Peninnah, *Chosen Tales: Stories Told by Jewish Storytellers* (Northvale, N.J.: Jason Aronson, Inc., 1995).

Schram, Peninnah, *Jewish Stories One Generation Tells Another* (Northvale, N.J.: Jason Aronson, Inc., 1989).

Silverman, William, *The Sages Speak: Rabbinical Wisdom and Jewish Values* (Northvale, N.J.: Jason Aronson, Inc., 1995).

Spaulding, Henry, *Encyclopedia of Jewish Humor* (New York: Jonathan David Publishers, 1969).

Telushkin, Joseph, *Jewish Wisdom* (New York: William Morrow and Company, 1994).

Weinreich, Beatrice Silverman, *Yiddish Folktales* (New York: Pantheon Books, 1988).

Wine, Sherwin, *Judaism Beyond God* (Farmington Hills, Michigan: Society for Humanistic Judaism, 1985).

Author's Note on Sources

My heavy reliance on Nathan Ausubel's *A Treasury Of Jewish Folklore* requires some explanation. After collecting the stories for this book, I researched Ausubel's background and discovered similarities to my own.

In 1948, the year *A Treasury of Jewish Folklore* was published, Nathan Ausubel was closely affiliated with the CPUSA, the American communist party. He had been a contributing editor of the communist journal *New Masses* and was currently a writer for the Yiddish communist daily the *Freiheit*.

In January 1948, the Communist Party press issued a pamphlet by Ausubel, "Jewish Culture in America: Weapon for Jewish Survival and Progress," in which he touted the achievements of the Soviet Union in nurturing a progressive Jewish culture and urged Americans to emulate them. This, of course, was pernicious nonsense. However he also argued insightfully that "although the main emphasis on Jewish culture in the past has been religious ... underneath it all, like a subterranean stream, flowed swiftly and strongly the affirmatively secular, the humane, the rational and the will to the good and just life for all men." He then cited selections from the Torah, the Prophets and the Talmud to prove his point. He ended his essay with a parable from the *Midrash* on the theme of uniting the weak to defeat the strong.

In 1953, Ausubel's next book appeared—*A Pictorial History of the Jewish People*. By then he recognized the anti-Semitic nature of the Soviet regime, without surrendering his attachment to secular, progressive Jewish values.

I come from a later generation of communist Jews—one that had already distanced itself from Stalinism. I grew up attending the Yiddish schools *(folkshuln)* originally established by the pro-communist Jewish Peoples' Fraternal Order (JPFO) and reading *Jewish Currents* magazine, which, until 1967, retained a residual loyalty to the Soviet Union. By my early teens (the mid-1960s), I already rejected the Soviet model in its entirety; however, I continued to think of myself as a socialist and a progressive Jew. As an adult, I joined the Congress of Secular Jewish Organizations (CSJO), in some ways a successor to the old JPFO, and in time became a regular contributor/columnist to *Jewish Currents* and its Canadian counterpart *Outlook*. In light of this history, I now understand why I was most drawn to Ausubel's selections. We were both searching for a "usable past" for secular progressive Jews.

Notwithstanding the merits of Ausubel's book, it poses a problem on a completely different level. He does not cite his sources or so much as include a bibliography. Although these shortcomings have not prevented *A Treasury of Jewish Folklore* from becoming the single most popular book on the subject, still in print 60 years after it was published, in the interests of good scholarship, for this new edition I have tracked down and provided the sources for all of Ausubel stories that come from Talmud and Midrash. His renditions often differ slightly from the original, but I too have adapted certain stories and I hope the reader will accept them as part of the ongoing process of creating Jewish folklore.

Original Sources
for Selections from Talmud and Midrash
Not Already Cited in the Text

p. 7   — Pirke Avot 1:18
p. 11   — based on Lamentations Rabbah 24
p. 12   — based on Babylonian Talmud, Sanhedrin 111a-b
p. 14   — based on Leviticus Rabbah 19:20
p. 18   — based on Babylonian Talmud, Ketubbot 77b
p. 21   — based on Babylonian Talmud, Baba Metzia 59a-59b
p. 25   — Pirke Avot 2:3 (Be cautious...)
p. 25   — Pirke Avot 5:11 (...justice delayed...)
p. 26   — based on Babylonian Talmud, Baba Metzia 83b-84a
p. 27   — based on Babylonian Talmud, Pesahim 25b, Sanhedrin
          74a
p. 28   — based on Babylonian Talmud, Avodah Zarah 18b
p. 36   — based on Babylonian Talmud, Shabbat 33b
p. 38   — based on Jerusalem Talmud, Sanhedrin 10, 27d-28a
          and Numbers Rabbah 7:19
p. 46   — based on Jerusalem Talmud, 2:5 (8C), Intro. to Tahuma
          Buber, 15:2, Pesikta De Rav Kahana, 9:1
p. 47   — based on Jerusalem Talmud, Terumot 8:10 and
          Genesis Rabbah, 94:9
p. 53   — Pirke Avot 1:14 (If I am not...)
p. 53   — Pirke Avot 3:22 (Rabban Yohanan...)
p. 54   — Pirke Avot 2:13 (In a place...)
p. 54   — Pirke Avot 2:6
p. 59   — based on Midrash Tanhuma 68
p. 63   — based on Intro. to Tanhuma, Buber 135
p. 67   — based on Babylonian Talmud, Taanit 22a

p. 82 — Pirke Avot 5:9
p. 83 — based on Babylonian Talmud, Yevamot 14b , Eruvin 13b, Berakhot 10b
p. 84 — based on the Babylonian Talmud, Shabbat 30b-31a
p. 86 — based on Babylonian Talmud, Hagigah 15b
p. 88 — based on Sanhedrin 109b, Numbers Rabbah 9:24, Genesis Rabbah 42:5,49:6, Leviticus Rabbah, 5:2, Pirkey de Rabbi Eliezer 25
p, 89 — Pirkey Avot (...plagues occur...)
p. 89 — based on Pesikta De Rav Kahana, 9:1 (Rabbi Joshua took...)
p. 91 — based on Babylonian Talmud, Baba Metzia 83a
p. 97 — based on Babylonian Talmud, Baba Metzia 86b
p. 106 — based on Leviticus Rabbah 34:10, Jerusalem Talmud, Pe'ah, 5-5, 21b, 8:9
p. 107 — The Fathers According to Rabbi Nathan 31b
p. 110 — based on Babylonian Talmud, Gittin 55b-57a, Genesis Rabbah 10:7, Lamentations Rabbah 1:15
p. 111 — based on Babylonian Talmud, Gittin 55b-57a, Genesis Rabbah 10:7, Lamentations Rabbah 1:15
p. 113 — based on Babylonian Talmud, Shabbat 33b
p. 139 — based on Alphabet of Ben Sira 23a-b, 33a-b (Lilith...)
p. 139 — based on Genesis Rabbah 70:19 (Leah...)
p. 156 — based on Babylonian Talmud, Rosh Hashanah 16b and Genesis Rabbah 53:9,14
p. 158 — based on Babylonian Talmud, Taanit 20a-b
p. 160 — based on Ecclesiastes Rabbah 28a
p. 162 — based on Tosafot on Babylonian Talmud, Avodah Zorah 10b
p. 164 — based on Babylonian Talmud, Avodah Zarah 10a-b
p. 166 — based on Babylonian Talmud, Kiddushin 31a (A pagan...)
p. 166 — based on Deuteronomy Rabbah 3:3, Jerusalem Talmud Ketubot 8:10 (Dealing honestly...)
p. 171 — based on Jerusalem Talmud, Shabbat 12:3, Horayot 3:5
p. 172 — based on Babylonian Talmud, Shabbat 119b

p. 174 — based on Midrash Tanhuma Mishpatim par. 2
              (Scholarship...)
p. 174 — based on Babylonian Talmud, Hagigah 15b, Jerusalem
              Talmud, Hagigah 77a-b (But there are alternatives...)
p. 188 — based on Babylonian Talmud, Nedarim, 40a,
p. 190 — based on Babylonian Talmud, Taanit 23a
p. 192 — based on Mishna Sanhedrin 4:5 and Babylonian
              Talmud, Sanhedrin 37a
p. 193 — based on Leviticus Rabbah 4:6
p. 196 — based on Babylonian Talmud, Taanit 8a
p. 197 — Pirke Avot, 1:10, 5:13, 2:5, 2:6,
p. 198 — Pirke Avot, 3:12, 2:21

Afterword

Secular Humanistic Judaism embraces a human-centered philosophy that affirms the power and responsibility of individuals to
shape their own lives independent of supernatural authority. It
maintains that ethics and morality should serve human needs —
chiefly, the preservation of human dignity and integrity — and that
behavior (ritual and otherwise) should reflect belief. Secular
Humanistic Jews value their Jewish identity and the aspects of
Jewish culture that offer a meaningful connection to the past and a
genuine expression of their contemporary way of life. Secular
Humanistic Jewish communities celebrate Jewish holidays and life
cycle events (such as weddings and bar and bat mitsva) with
inspirational ceremonies that draw upon, but are not limited to, traditional literature.

Secular Humanistic Judaism is a growing force within North
America today. Meeting the needs of those who seek a Judaism
consistent with their contemporary lifestyle and values, providing a
Judaism that is compatible with the secular perspective of young
people today, offering a meaningful way for those who identify
themselves as "just Jewish" to celebrate their Jewish identity, providing a welcoming environment for the intermarried to affirm their
attachment to Jewish culture and community, creating a path back
to Judaism for the unaffiliated who do not join traditional communities, Secular Humanistic Judaism is the best hope for Jewish survival in the twenty-first century.

The International Institute for Secular Humanistic Judaism is the
educational arm of the International Federation of Secular
Humanistic Jews, an association of national organizations from

the United States, Canada, Israel, Belgium, France, Great Britain, Italy, Australia, Argentina, Uruguay, Mexico, and the countries of the former Soviet Union. As the intellectual and teaching center of the movement, the Institute sponsors programs in Israel, Eurasia, and throughout North America for professional and lay leaders, educators, and individuals interested in learning more about Secular Humanistic Judaism and trains rabbis, leaders, cantors, and educators.

The Institute's commitment to Jewish identity and continuity forms the foundation of its programs. Secular Humanistic Judaism sees pluralism as the best guarantee of Jewish survival. By training rabbis, leaders, cantors, and educators for communities, by publishing philosophical and celebrational texts, by offering adult outreach and children's programs to the world Jewish community, the Institute serves as a positive force for the continuation of the Jewish people, enriching life for all Jews.

To learn more about Secular Humanistic Judaism, contact:

International Institute for Secular Humanistic Judaism
28611 West Twelve Mile Road
Farmington Hills, MI 48334
248-476-9532
info@IISHJ.org
http://www.iishj.org